Retire The Right Way

with the Dynamic Duo

Nancy & Jamie
BLUMENTHAL

Growing and Protecting Family Wealth

This document discusses general concepts for retirement planning, and is not intended to provide tax or legal advice. Individuals are urged to consult with their tax and legal professionals regarding these issues.

Printed in the United States of America

First Printing, 2014

Gradient Positioning Systems, LLC
4105 Lexington Avenue North, Suite 110
Arden Hills, MN 55126 (877) 901-0894

Table of Contents

Acknowledgments

First and foremost, we would like to thank our parents for instilling in us a strong work ethic and moral obligation. The lessons we learned from our parents have allowed the door to success to swing open, and for that we are eternally grateful. To our children, Stephanie and Nathan, thank your for your love, support, and inspiration. Family is at the core of all we do, and to our clients we thank all of you for allowing us to serve you, and being a part of our extended family. Finally, we would like to thank the contributions of Nick Stovall, Mike Binger, Nate Lucius and Gradient Positioning Systems, LLC.

Nancy & Jamie

Introduction

*Mark and Marie have been busy. During the last 30 years they have worked to pay the bills, keep up with the house payments, and raise two kids. They financed the cost of braces and birthday parties, outfits and swimming lessons, Disneyland. They invested in eight years worth of hockey equipment and cheerleading and traveling to and from the games; day camps, weekend camps, and summer camps. After that came the college applications and road trips and decorating the dorm room, the mini-fridge and the rug, and the new laptop computer. Their daughter, Natalie, goes to a state college for $25,000 a year; their son, Nathan, moved a little further from home at $50,000 a year. Mark and Marie have been saving for retirement, tucking away a portion of their paychecks into a 401(k) and an IRA. They draw on these funds to help pay for their kid's college tuition. Their kids graduate, ready to start their young professional lives, and there comes the day when Mark and Marie look at each other realize: **we're here.***

Mark is 58 and Marie is 56. They are nearing their retirement years, and about to enter a new phase of their lives, yet a part of them never really believed they would get to this part. Here they are, in their fifties, the kids grown and off to college. Are they ready to retire? They look at what is left of their savings and they wonder, can we make it? Do we have enough to live on? And what's more, do we have enough to live the way we are used to living?

UNPRECEDENTED CHALLENGES FACE AMERICA'S PRE-AND-POST RETIREES

Our parents had what was probably the best and the most comfortable middle-class retirement available: a pension with a $4,000 a month retirement check, a Social Security benefit of $2,000 per spouse, and a house they bought and paid for. Unfortunately, those days are gone. Today's pre-and-post retirees face unprecedented challenges brought about by several factors, most of them outside of their control. The new 401(k) plans offered by employers have shifted the onus of retirement savings onto the shoulders of the workers, and those savings typically only account for about 25 percent of their retirement needs. If you are age 55 or younger, Social Security is a benefit you may not be able to count on, and even if you do have it available to you now, it will supply, on average, about 39 percent of your income needs.* Where does the rest of the money come from, and who is responsible for structuring this money to form a reliable income stream? The answer is a short one: You.

Retirement today is a self-directed and self-implemented enterprise. If you are like Mark and Marie, wondering how you got here and worried about how to make ends meet during the next 20 or 30 years, you are going to need some guidance. Not only

---

*http://www.ssa.gov/pressoffice/basicfact.htm

should you expect to live longer than your parents did – 19 years longer for men and 15 years longer for women according to the Social Security Administration* – but the global economy and government debt-reduction buyouts have made the stock market an increasingly risky place to grow and hold your retirement nest egg. The alternative – putting your money in safe vehicles such as bonds and certificates of deposit (CDs) – can't keep up with inflation and in some cases, after taxes, even results in negative earnings. This poses a tough dilemma for retirees seeking a way to turn their savings into a reliable, protected, and flexible income stream that can support them during their retirement years.

The fear of running out of money is a real concern. It can happen and it has happened to the many retirees who lost hundreds of thousands of dollars during the stock market downturns of 2008 and 2009, and as a result, faced the dilemma of delaying retirement, going back to work, and rebuilding their savings all over again. *You don't control what the annual return on your assets will be once they are invested, but you CAN control how your money is growing by transitioning those assets.* As you near or enter the retirement phase of your life – this wonderful time in your life that you've worked so hard for – the first and perhaps most important transition you have to make begins with your own mindset.

TRANSITIONING FROM THE ACCUMULATION STAGE TO THE PRESERVATION STAGE

During your working years, you work, you save, and you pay off debt. As your money grows in the investment vehicles you have chosen, there are no regular withdrawals, and any losses due to stock market corrections are mitigated by time and the steady influx of deposits coming from your paycheck. Once you enter

---

*http://www.ncbi.nlm.nih.gov/books/NBK62373/

into your retirement years, however, all that changes. When you stop working, there are no more steady paychecks, and no more deposits going into your savings account. What happens now is you start to take that money out. You make a transition from what is known as *the accumulation stage* of life to *the preservation stage* because now, that money you have worked so hard to save *must support you*. But how do you preserve and structure those funds so they can do that?

Many people make the mistake of thinking they won't need as much income once they retire and are no longer working. But take a minute to think about all the things you've been wanting to do during your retirement years. Travelling, trips with the grandkids, buying that RV. Retirement will afford you much more time to do all the things you've always wanted to do, but those activities come with a price tag. Most people need about 70 percent of their workforce income during their retirement years.* Moving into the preservation stage of your life begins with structuring an income to ensure the investments you've made over the years can sustain and support you for the years to come, funding and supporting all of your retirement activities.

Most people have three pressing concerns when it comes to their retirement income:

- *Will I have enough income to live the lifestyle I'm accustomed to?*
- *How will I pay for long term health care if I get sick?*
- *Do I want to leave money for my loved ones as a legacy?*

The right financial tools will give you the peace of mind that comes from having a protected, flexible and guaranteed income. Structuring that income is a big part of retirement planning, but it isn't the only concern. Retiring the right way can be compared

---

http://money.cnn.com/2012/07/12/pf/expert/preretirement-income.moneymag/index.htm

to the icon many have come to associate with the ideal of the retirement years: the cozy comfy easy chair.

THE FOUR LEGS OF YOUR RETIREMENT CHAIR

Planning for retirement the right way begins with a solid legal and financial foundation. Think of it like the four legs of chair: if you take away any one of the chair legs, what happens? The chair topples over. It might look okay from across the room, but as soon as you put any weight on it, it falls. The same thing can happen to your retirement dream if it's not stabilized by each of the four legs. Each one of the four legs of the chair represents one of four areas of your retirement plan:

Estate Planning: How do you protect and secure your retirement savings? Is it possible to organize your nest egg in such a way so that it can continue to lay the golden eggs, and not just for your income, but for the good of family members and loved ones for years to come? Your retirement income can be divided into two kinds of money: Live On and Leave On money. The Live On money is structured to provide you with an income that keeps up with the lifestyle you've grown accustomed to. The Leave On money can be used to fund large purchases down the road, cover the costs of long term health care needs, and provide a legacy for your family.

Financial Planning: How do you structure an income that keeps up with the rate of inflation? Financial planning is all about the income and growth. You want the principal of your nest egg to be guaranteed and protected from market risk, while at the same time allowing for some growth of principal. Is there a financial tool available that can give you growth, protection and flexibility? Is it possible to create an income stream that is self-managing and perpetual so that you don't need to pay a broker to manage it for you? Today's new equity indexed annuities might be the right financial tool for you.

Taxes: We all have to pay taxes, but paying more taxes than you have to can significantly erode your retirement savings. This book will address the dilemma of Social Security taxation, earned interest income, and the taxation of your legacy benefits in retirement savings vehicles such as traditional IRAs.

Health Care and Legacy Planning: The Congressional Budget Office has labeled the cost of long term care "*the greatest unfunded liability in America today.*" Not planning for the inevitability issues of health care expenses can devastate your retirement nest egg and drastically reduce your legacy benefits. Learn about advanced planning strategies and tools that allow you to protect what you've accumulated and maximize your gifts to family, loved ones or your favorite charity.

RETIREMENT AND THE THREE BEARS

You have worked hard all of your life to accumulate your retirement savings. How much of these assets do you want exposed to risk? How much of your hard-earned money do you want to leave unprotected? How much can you stand to lose? It's alright to say, "None of it." ***You want to protect it all.*** This is where we come in. Retirement Strategies and Solutions can help you organize your assets, develop an income plan for safety, security, and growth, and provide you with support for the long term so all the issues that can sabotage your happy retirement are addressed. Nobody wants to think about things like taxes, inflation, and getting sick. These are the three retirement bears that can really ruin a good time. Retiring the right way means looking each of those bears right in the eye, addressing the problem, and finding a solution that is 'just right' before any damage is done. As the President and founder of Retirement Strategies and Solutions, I can tell you that the right financial tools are out there and available to you. We have a team of professionals waiting here to help. All you need to do is get over the hurdle of the biggest bear of all – procrastination bear.

THE BLUMENTHAL TEAM

We know how hard it is to face the realities of retirement planning. We understand firsthand the challenges, the fears, and the struggles that come from raising a family and supporting a marriage. My wife and I have been through it all together, married 30 years, working and raising our own two kids. It is our mission and our passion to understand and support the retirement goals important to you and your family. We hope this book can serve as a valuable resource to get you started on the design of your living roadmap to the retirement you've earned. As a team, we welcome the opportunity to address your needs, and help you find solutions to your retirement challenges. We understand where you've been, and we're here to help you get to where you want to go. When you work with us, you're one of the family.

1

Plan Right, Retire Right

"No one plans to fail, they just fail to plan."

Miles and Gloria are talking about retirement. They want to retire when they are 65, but Gloria doesn't think they have enough money saved. Miles has been putting away 7 percent of his income into a company 401(k) but feels he should be saving closer to 12 percent. Gloria doesn't have a company 401(k) plan but does have her own IRA. She is in charge of the household finances and paying the bills, and Miles often accuses her of not putting enough money away into savings. She tries to explain to him that there is always an expense that comes up. When they sit down to talk about their retirement plans, they end up blaming each other for not having enough money put away and arguing about who spends how much on what and when. These conversations aren't very productive. Gloria and Miles are talking about retirement, but they aren't any closer to having a plan.

Talking about money isn't always easy. No one wants to be judged or told they aren't saving enough. This anxiety and embarrassment causes many pre-retirees to put off seeking the help of a financial professional to talk about their retirement plan. According to one study from the National Seniors Productive Ageing Centre, a research group based in Melbourne, Australia, and co-authored by an American professor, nearly half of the participants reported "mild" anxiety about the prospect of talking with a financial professional, and one in four participants described their anxiety as "moderate" to "severe."*

It's natural to have these feelings about money, because these numbers are attached to the people and circumstances of your life. It is personal. In many ways, talking with a financial professional about your retirement plans is like seeking the help of a medical doctor. It might not be all good news, but in going to the appointment, you will at least find out exactly what you are dealing with. Your professional can examine your assets and liabilities, and help put together a retirement plan that you can live by. Yes, they may make some recommendations that you might not be all too excited about – just like your doctor who is telling you to cut back on the beer – but talking about it and creating a plan will ultimately give you greater peace of mind.

THE RETIREMENT TALK

Before sitting down with your financial professional, it's important to talk with your spouse, partner or loved one about your retirement plans. As in the story example of Miles and Gloria above, talking about money can be an emotional subject. It may help to take a step back from the finances and start with the more personal components of your retirement plan. Make it a fun evening out

*http://www.usatoday.com/story/money/columnist/powell/2014/02/22/financial-adviser-retirement/5555275/

over dinner or drinks. Start by asking each other questions about what you hope to do during your retirement years.

- Are you wanting to start a business?
- Take up a new hobby?
- Begin a second career?
- And what about lifestyle changes? Would moving to a more rural area make sense during retirement? Do you want to be closer to the grandkids?

Answering questions like this can often have a significant impact on the financial side of things as well. For example, the expenses of living in big city can be twice that of living in a rural area. Maybe down-sizing to a smaller apartment makes sense in more ways than one. Or maybe your spouse would like to turn the garage into a studio. Planning on how you will enjoy the new and often greater amounts of time you have to spend together is also an important part of the conversation.

Once you have an understanding of what's important to each other, it's time to take a look at the numbers. Instead of pointing the blame, come together as a team with the unified objective of achieving those goals and ideas that are so important to each of you. Take a look at your expenses for the last six months to get an idea of the amount of income you will need during your retirement. Think of those numbers as neutral things – neither good nor bad, but just what they are. If one partner is more in-volved than the other when it comes to finances, this is the time to get that person up to speed. You both want to be involved and informed about where your assets are, and what those investments can and should do for the security of your future.

WHERE DO YOU WANT TO BE?

Today's retirees have redefined what it means to be retired. Answers to the question, '***What do you want to do during retirement?***'

are as varied as the individual, spanning the gambit from sitting in the easy chair to starting a new company. What are your answers to the question: **Where Do You Want to Be?**

Before you can plan for where you are going, you have to know exactly where you stand today. Taking stock of your assets begins with an examination of the monthly expenses. Group those expenses into one of two categories:

- *Essential*: expenses such as food, housing, car insurance, etc.
- *Discretionary*: expenses such as dining out, travel and entertainment, etc.

After examining your expenses, it's time to take a look at your assets. Inventory all your holdings and assets that could serve as potential sources for income. Look at all your investments including tax-qualified plans such as 401(k)s, 403(b)s and IRAs.

Structuring assets to create an income-generating retirement requires a different approach than earning income via the workforce. Saving money for retirement, which is what you have spent your life doing, and *planning* your retirement are two different things. Both are important. Add to the planning of retirement the complexities of taxes, required minimum distributions (RMDs) from IRAs and legacy planning, and you can begin to see why happy endings require more than hope. They need a focused and well-executed plan.

Understanding how to manage your assets entails risk management, risk diversification, tax planning and income planning preparation throughout your life stages. These strategies can help you leverage more from each one of the hard-earned dollars you set aside for your retirement. Perhaps the most important lessons investors learned from the Great Recession is that not understanding where your money is invested (and the potential risks of those investments) can work against you, your plans for retirement and your legacy. Saving and investing money isn't enough to truly get the most out of it. You must have a planful approach to managing your assets.

Essentially, managing your money and your investments is an ongoing process that requires customization and adaptation to a changing world. And make no mistake; the world is always changing. What worked for your parents or even your parents' parents was probably good advice back then. People in retirement or approaching retirement today need new ideas and professional guidance. They also need a plan. Your plan starts with a conversation about where you want to go. What do you want these years of your life to mean to you? What do you hope to do? And who do you want to spend your time with? Once you understand your objectives and know your financial situation as it stands today, we can begin leveraging the right financial tools to help you achieve the ideal of where you to be.

HOPE SO VS. KNOW SO MONEY

Designing a retirement plan is all about choosing the right financial tools that can help you get from where you are now to where you want to go. Not all financial tools are created equal. Some tools are designed for growth, others for protection, and other tools can do a little bit of both. Understanding whether or not an investment is right for you begins with an understanding of the basic truths about money as it relates to saving for retirement.

There are essentially two ways to describe the money in your financial investments: *Hope So* and *Know So*. Everyone can divide their money into these two categories. Some have more of one kind than the other, and there is nothing inherently bad about either type. The goal isn't to eliminate one kind of money but to understand the two types of money and then balance them as you approach retirement.

Hope So Money is money that is at risk. It fluctuates with the market. It has no minimum guarantee. It is subject to investor activity, stock prices, market trends, buying trends, etc. You get the picture. This money is exposed to more risk but also has the potential for more reward. Because the market is subject to change, you can't really be sure what the value of your investments will be worth in the future. You can't really *rely* on it at all. For this reason, we refer to it as Hope So Money. This doesn't mean you shouldn't have some money invested in the market, but it would be dangerous to assume you can know what it will be worth in the future.

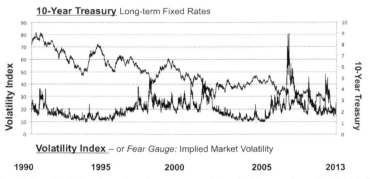

10-Year Treasury Long-term Fixed Rates

Volatility Index – or *Fear Gauge:* Implied Market Volatility

| 1990 | 1995 | 2000 | 2005 | 2013 |

Source: Yahoo Finance – 12-31-2013. VIX is a trademarked ticker symbol for the Chicago Board Options Exchange Market Volatility Index, a popular measure of the implied volatility of S&P 500 index options. Often referred to as the fear index or the fear gauge, it represents one measure of the market's expectation of stock market volatility over the next 30 day period (wikipedia.com). The CBOE 10-year Treasury Note (TNX) is based on 10 times the yield-to-maturity on the most recently auctioned 10-year Treasury note. Past performance does not guarantee future results. Some illustrators may show how a market index has performed. An investor cannot invest in an index, although there are some investments designed to mirror index performance. Past performance is not a guarantee of future results.

The VIX, or volatility index, of the market represents expected market volatility. When the VIX drops, economic experts expect less volatility. When the VIX rises, more volatility is expected.

1. *VIX is a trademarked ticker symbol for the Chicago Board Options Exchange (CBOE) Market Volatility Index, a popular measure of the implied volatility of S&P 500 index options. Often referred to as the fear index or the fear gauge, it represents one measure of the market's expectation of stock market volatility over the next 30 day period. (wikipedia.com)*

2. *The CBOE 10-Year Treasury Note (TNX) is based on 10 times the yield-to-maturity on the most recently auctioned 10-year Treasury note.*

Hope So Money is an important element of a retirement plan, especially in the early stages of planning when you can trade volatility for potential returns, and when a longer investment timeframe is available to you. In the long run, time can smooth out the ups and downs of money exposed to the market. Working with a professional and leveraging a long-term investment strategy has the potential to create rewarding returns from Hope So Money.

Know So Money, on the other hand, is safer when compared to Hope So Money. Know So Money is made up of dependable, low-risk or no-risk money, and investments that you can count on. Social Security is one of the most common forms of Know So Money. Income you draw or will draw from Social Security is guaranteed. You have paid into Social Security your entire career, and you can rely on that money during your retirement. Unlike the market, rates of growth for Know So Money are dependent on 10-year treasury rates. The 10-year treasury, or TNX, is commonly considered to represent a very secure and safe place for your money, hence Know So Money. The 10-year treasury drives key rates for things such as mortgage rates or CD rates. Know So Money may not be as exciting as Hope So Money, but it is safer. You can safely be fairly sure you will have it in the future.

Knowing the difference between Hope So and Know So Money is an important step towards a successful retirement plan. People who are 55 or older and who are looking ahead to retirement should be relying on more Know So Money than Hope So Money.

Ideally, the rates of return on Hope So and Know So Money would have an overlapping area that provided an acceptable rate of risk for both types of money. In the early 1990s, interest rates were high and market volatility was low. At that time, you could invest in either Hope So or Know So Money options because the rates of return were similar from both Know So and Hope So investments, and you were likely to be fairly successful with a wide range of investment options. At that time, you could expose yourself to an acceptable amount of risk or an acceptable fixed rate. Basically, it was difficult to make a mistake during that time period. Today, you don't have those options. Market volatility is at all-time highs while interest rates are at all-time lows. They are so far apart from each other that it is hard to know what to do with your money.

Yesterday's investment rules may not work today. Not only could they hamper achieving your goals, they may actually harm your financial situation. We are currently in a period when the rates for Know So Money options are at historic lows, and the volatility of Hope So Money is higher than ever. There is no overlapping acceptable rate, making both options less than ideal. *Because of this uncertain financial landscape, wise investment strategies are more important now than ever.*

This unique situation requires fresh ideas and investment tools that haven't been relied on in the past. Investing the way your parents did will not pay off. The majority of investment ideas used by financial professionals in the 1990s aren't applicable to today's markets. That kind of investing will likely get you in trouble and compromise your retirement. Today, you need a better PLAN.

HOW MUCH RISK ARE *YOU* EXPOSED TO?

Many investors don't know how much risk they are exposed to. It is helpful to organize your assets so you can have a clear understanding of how much of your money is at risk and how much is in safer holdings. This process starts with listing all your assets.

Let's take a look at the two kinds of money:

Hope So Money is, as the name indicates, money that you *hope* will be there when you need it. Hope So Money represents what you would like to get out of your investments. Examples of Hope So Money include:

- Stock market funds, including index funds
- Mutual funds
- Variable annuities
- REITS

Know So Money is money that you know you can count on. It is safer money that isn't exposed to the level of volatility as the asset types noted above. You can more confidently count on having this money when you need it. Examples of Know So Money are:
- Government backed bonds
- Savings and checking accounts
- Fixed income annuities
- CDs
- Treasuries
- Money market accounts

> » *Charlie had a modest brokerage account that he added to when he could. When he changed jobs a couple years ago, at age 58, Charlie transferred his 401(k) assets into an IRA. Just a few years from retirement, he is now beginning to realize that nearly every dollar he has saved for retirement is subject to market risk.*
>
> *Intuitively, Charlie knows that the time has come to shift some assets out of accumulation-focused investment vehicles and into an alternative that is safer and more focused on the preservation of his assets. But how much is the right amount?*

WHAT IS MY RISK NUMBER?

Determining the amount of risk that is right for you is dependent on a number of variables. You need to feel comfortable with where and how you are investing your money, and your financial professional is obligated to help you make decisions that put your money in places that fit your risk criteria.

Your retirement needs to first accommodate your day-to-day income needs. How much money do you need to maintain your lifestyle? When do you need it?

Managing your risk by having a balance of Hope So Money vs. Know So Money is a good start that will put you ahead of the curve. But how much Know So Money is enough to secure your income needs during retirement, and how much Hope So Money is enough to allow you to continue to benefit from an improving market?

In short, how do you begin to know how much risk you should be exposed to?

While there is no single approach to investment risk determination advice that is universally applicable to everyone, there are some helpful guidelines. One of the most useful is called *The Rule of 100*.

The average investor needs to accumulate assets to create a retirement plan that provides income during retirement and also allows for legacy planning. To accomplish this, they need to balance the amount of risk to which they are exposed. Risk is required because, while Know So Money is safer, more reliable and more dependable, it doesn't grow very fast, if at all. Today's historically low interest rates barely break even with current inflation. Hope So Money, while less dependable, has more potential for growth. Hope So Money can eventually become Know So Money once you move it to an investment with lower risk. Everyone's risk diversification will be different depending on their goals, age and their existing assets.

So how do you decide how much risk your assets should be exposed to? Where do you begin? Luckily, there's a guideline you can use to start making decisions about risk management. It's called the Rule of 100.

THE RULE OF 100

The Rule of 100 is a general rule that helps shape asset diversification* for the average investor. The rule states that the number 100 minus an investor's age equals the amount of assets they should have exposed to risk.

The Rule of 100: 100 - (your age) = the percentage of your assets that should be exposed to risk (Hope So Money)

For example, if you are a 30-year-old investor, the Rule of 100 would indicate that you should be focusing on investing primarily in the market and taking on a substantial amount of risk in your portfolio. The Rule of 100 suggests that 70 percent of your investments should be exposed to risk.

100 - (30 years of age) = 70 percent

Now, not every 30-year-old should have exactly 70 percent of their assets in mutual funds and stocks. The Rule of 100 is based on your chronological age, not your "financial age," which could vary based on your investment experience, your aversion

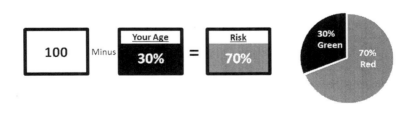

*Asset Diversification disclosure – Diversification and asset allocation does not assure of guarantee better performance and cannot eliminate the risk of investment loss. Before investing, you should carefully read the applicable volatility disclosure for each of the underlying funds, which can be found in the current prospectus.

or acceptance of risk and other factors. While this rule isn't an ironclad solution to anyone's finances, it's a pretty good place to start. Once you've taken the time to look at your assets with a professional to determine your risk exposure, you can use the Rule of 100 to make changes that put you in a more stable investment position — one that reflects your comfort level.

Perhaps when you were age 30 and starting your career, as in the example above, it made sense to have 70 percent of your money in the market: you had time on your side. You had plenty of time to save more money, work more and recover from a downturn in the market. Retirement was ages away, and your earning power was increasing. And indeed, younger investors should take on more risk for exactly those reasons. The potential reward of long-term involvement in the market outweighs the risk of investing when you are young.

Risk tolerance generally reduces as you get older, however. If you are 40 years old and lose 30 percent of your portfolio in a market downturn this year, you have 20 or 30 years to recover it. If you are 68 years old, you have five to 10 years (or less) to make the same recovery. That new circumstance changes your whole retirement perspective. At age 68, it's likely that you simply aren't as interested in suffering through a tough stock market. There is less time to recover from downturns, and the stakes are higher. The money you have saved is money you will soon need to provide you with income, or is money that you already need to meet your income demands.

Much of the flexibility that comes with investing earlier in life is related to *compounding*. Compounded earnings can be incredibly powerful over time. The longer your money has time to compound, the greater your wealth will be. This is what most people talk about when they refer to putting their money to work. This is also why the Rule of 100 favors risk for the young. If you start investing when you are young, you can invest smaller amounts of money in a more aggressive fashion because you have the potential to make a profit in a rising market and you can harness the power of compounding earnings. When you are 40, 50 or 60 years old, that potential becomes less and less and you are forced to have more money at lower amounts of risk to realize the same returns. It basically becomes more expensive to prudently invest the older you get.

You risk not having a recovery period the older you get, so should have less of your assets at risk in volatile investments. You should shift with the Rule of 100 to protect your assets and ensure that they will provide you with the income you need in retirement. Let's look at another example that illustrates how the Rule of 100 becomes more critical as you age. An 80-year-old investor who is retired and is relying on retirement assets for income, for example, needs to depend on a solid amount of Know So Money. The Rule of 100 says an 80-year-old investor should have a maximum of 20 percent of his or her assets at risk. Depending on the investor's financial position, even less risk exposure may be required. You are the only person who can make this kind of determination, but the Rule of 100 can help. Everyone has their own level of comfort. Your Rule of 100 results will be based on your values and attitudes as well as your comfort with risk.

The Rule of 100 can apply to overarching financial management and to specific investment products that you own as well. Take the 401(k) for example. Many people have them, but not many people understand how their money is allocated within their 401(k). An employer may have someone who comes in once a year and explains the models and options that employees can choose from, but that's as much guidance as most 401(k) holders get. Many 401(k) options include target date funds that change their risk exposure over time, essentially following a form of the Rule of 100. Selecting one of these options can often be a good move for employees because they shift your risk as you age, securing more Know So Money when you need it.

TURNING HOPE SO INTO KNOW SO

A financial professional can look at your assets with you and discuss alternatives to optimize your balance between Know So and Hope So Money. The fact of the matter is that a lot of people don't know their level of exposure to risk. Organizing your assets according to Hope So and Know So money is an important and powerful way to get a clear picture of what kind of money you have, where it is and how you can best use it in the future. This process is as simple as listing your assets and assigning them a status based on Know So or Hope So Money. Work with your financial professional to create a comprehensive inventory of your assets to understand what you are working with before making any decisions. This may be the first time you have ever sat down and sorted out all of your assets, allowing you to see how much money you have at risk in the market. Comparing the risk inherent in your investments will give you an idea of how near or far you are from adhering to the Rule of 100.

CHAPTER 1 RECAP //

- Talking about money can be an unpleasant and anxiety-producing subject. Before meeting with your financial professional, take the time to have *the retirement talk* with your spouse or loved ones. What is it you hope to be doing? Where would you like to live? Is there a move in your future? A new business or hobby? Taking the time to have this conversation can help ease into the monetary side of things, making budgetary issues more pertinent to your goals and objectives.

- Monthly expenditures can be divided into two categories: essential and discretionary. Essential expenses include paying the bills for utilities; discretionary expenses are the fun things you hope to be able to do.

- Your assets can also be organized into two different categories of money: Hope So and Know So. Hope So Money is money you hope you'll have in the future, and Know So Money is money you know you'll have in the future.

- Organizing your assets starts with making a list and understanding which investments have the potential to generate Hope So Money and which generate Know So Money. Your exposure to risk is ultimately determined by you.

- Use the Rule of 100 as a general guiding principle when determining how much risk your retirement investments should be exposed to (100 - [your age] = [percentage of your investments that can comfortably exposed to risk]).

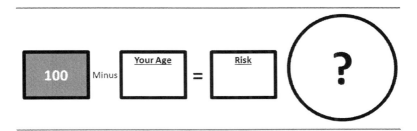

2

Live On and Leave On Money

"Can we live the same kind of lifestyle in retirement that we've grown accustomed to?"

Mr. Chip is 58 years old with a portfolio that was once valued at $892,000. He took a hit during the stock market correction of 2008, and in hopes of recapturing that loss, he kept his money in the market in the years leading up to his retirement. He didn't have a concrete plan, but hoped to retire sometime around age 65. Unfortunately for Mr. Chip, the stock market doesn't perform well and for the next three years he takes a significant hit. Mr. Chip doesn't retire at age 62 but instead keeps working. He leaves his money in the market, doesn't take any out and lets his account grow. Assuming a 6 percent rate of return, his account value at the end of 11 years is $292,000.

Mr. Chip is now 69 ½, and ready to retire. But will he have enough money to keep the lifestyle he is accustomed to?

Mr. Sweet is also 58-years old with an investment portfolio that was also once valued at $892,000. He also took a hit during 2008 and decides that he's done with the market. He doesn't want his retirement savings to be sitting at risk, but he's also worried that he won't have enough money after taking such a loss. Five years before retiring, Mr. Sweet seeks the guidance of a financial professional. He learns about diversifying his portfolio, and moves a portion of his assets into a Know So indexed annuity investment structured for a guaranteed income. When he is ready, Mr. Sweet retires, and starts taking out $30,000 of income every year for the next 11 years. Meanwhile, his investment continues to grow in the annuity and earns the same 6 percent rate of return as his neighbor, Mr. Chip, only Mr. Sweet doesn't take any of the market hits because of the annuity's guarantee of principal. At the end of 11 years and at age 69 1/2, Mr. Sweet has an account value that is $562,830.*

Today's retirement poses a difficult challenge for retirees. Your assets must be coordinated to supply a steady income stream, but at the same time, those assets must continue to grow so they can last your lifetime. Failing to allocate your assets can result in running out of money, as in the example story above with Mr. Chip. Most people want to continue enjoying the same standard of living they currently have during their retirement years. They can also expect

---

*This hypothetical example is for illustrative purposes only and is not a prediction or guarantee of actual results which will vary from those described. This example isn't intended to represent the value or performance of a specific product. The retirement vehicle in this example is assumed to be tax-deferred, so taxes are not paid until withdrawals are made. Annual withdrawals do not reflect the impact of taxes or inflation. Some retirement vehicles have charges, fees or expenses which are not reflected and which would lower the amounts available for withdrawal.

to live longer than their parents did, which means future expenses have to be planned for, 10, 20 and even 30 years down the road. Your retirement plan must take into account your expenses for tomorrow, but because this is money you *know* you will need, risk-oriented Hope So investments such as stock market funds may not be the best choice.

If you only take away one thing from reading this book, the most important thing to realize is this: ***it is the years just before and just after retirement that your savings are at their most vulnerable***. Why? Because taking a loss due to stock market fluctuations during those years can significantly damage your portfolio's ability to sustain you during the long term. This is due to something known as the "sequence of returns" which basically dictates that it's not so much the size of the loss, but *when that loss occurs*. Two investors can have the exact same portfolio amounts averaging the same rate of return, but if investor A incurs significant loss during the first three years of his retirement, followed by gain, he or she will have less money than the investor who incurs the exact same losses and gains but in a different order.

Timing is everything. If you do nothing else, it is crucial you address the issue of asset allocation as soon as you retire or, for best results, when retirement is a good three to five years out.

The foundation of income planning begins with structuring your assets so they can provide you with an income today that keeps pace with inflation tomorrow. You also want your money protected against the market downturns and you want flexibility, because we all know that life happens and things come up. In addition to identifying the risk of your investments in Hope So and Know So terms, it can also be helpful to organize your assets according to what you want that money to do for you.

YOUR MONEY TREE

Our parents often told us as children that money doesn't grow on trees, but let's take a minute and imagine that it does. If you think of your retirement in terms of a big tree bearing the fruit of your hard-earned dollar bills, imagine how you will need to pick some of that money now. This is what can be thought of as Live On Money. You need it for income, bills, and various day-to-day expenses. You want that money to be readily available, like apples on a tree. Most likely these funds will be kept in a liquid account such as checking or savings, because you want to be able to access this money without having to call up your financial professional.

But there's also another kind of money, and maybe even another kind of tree altogether. This is a tree that you plant today and let grow for tomorrow. You might keep an eye on that tree and keep it protected from wild animals. This is your Leave On Money. You want to leave this tree alone and give it time to mature so it will bear fruit for you later on, when you need it. Leave On money can be used for larger expenses down the road such as a new vehicle, house repairs, and the cost of long term health care. It might also be what you want to leave the grandkids as a legacy asset to pass on at your demise. Leave On money includes death benefits from Life Insurance policies and stretch IRAs.

Leave On Money is used for accumulation. It's money that you don't need now for income, but will need to rely on down the road. It's still considered Know So Money because you will rely on it later for income or other expenses such as long term care and as such you will need to count on it being there. Leave On Money also represents income your assets will need to generate for future use. For example, you may structure some Leave On money during pre-retirement, while you are still working. There are newer types of annuities, such as those used by Mr. Sweet in the example story above, that can provide a guaranteed income stream at a time pre-determined by you. When you don't need that money to Live On, it can be growing for you – out of sight, out of mind – accumulating enough interest to provide you with an additional two to three thousand dollars a month.

It's vital to the success of your retirement planning to decide how much of your assets to structure for Live On Money now and how much to set aside to accumulate and grow for Leave On Money later. Your Live On money needs come first. It is the Live On money that will dictate how much money will be left over to plant for future Leave On Money needs.

LIVE ON MONEY: YOUR INCOME

An important aspect of your financial plan is the evaluation of your income needs. Finding the most efficient and beneficial way to address them will have impacts on your lifestyle, your asset accumulation and your legacy planning after you retire. Satisfying that need for daily income entails first knowing *how much you need* and *when you will need it.*

How Much Money Do You Need? While this amount will be different for everyone, the general rule of thumb is that a retiree will require 70 to 80 percent of their pre-retirement income to maintain their lifestyle. Once you know what that number is, the key becomes matching your income need with the correct investment strategies, options and tools to satisfy that need.

When Do You Need Your Money? If you need income to last 10 years, use a financial tool designed to create just that. If you need a lifetime of income, seek a tool that will do that while providing protection and a guarantee of principal.

So how do you figure out how much you need and when you need it? When you take health care costs, potential emergencies, plans for moving or traveling, and other retirement expenses into account, you can really give your calculator a workout. You want to maximize retirement benefits to meet your lifetime income needs. As we determined earlier in Chapter 1, creating an income plan begins with the retirement talk and understanding just what it is you want that money to be able to do for you. Some people file for Social Security on day one of their retirement. Others rely on supplemental income from an IRA or another retirement account. A financial professional can help you answer those questions by working with you to customize an income plan.

LEAVE ON MONEY: ESTATE PLANNING AND YOUR ASSETS

Estate planning isn't just for the wealthy. As you enter into your retirement years, it's vital to your financial health that you take the time to structure your assets so they can go to work for you, both in the short-term and in the long-term. Establishing an income plan to provide you with a steady supply of Live On Money is one aspect of estate planning. Defining who will inherit your assets and determining guardianship of any minor children is another aspect, particularly if you have dependents with special needs. Creating an optimal strategy for your estate is also about more than just managing estate tax, it's about organizing your assets so they pass on to your family, loved ones or a charity in the manner you wish. It's about maximizing how much you leave behind, while still ensuring that your financial needs are taken care of for the rest of your life. Estate planning is a big-picture approach to the management of your assets.

Over the course of your lifetime, it is likely that you have acquired a variety of assets. Assets can range from money that you have in a savings account or a 401(k), to a pension or an IRA. You have earned money and have made financial decisions based on the best information you had at the time. When viewed as a whole, however, you might not have an overall strategy for the management of your assets. As we have seen, it's more important than ever to know which of your assets are at risk. High market volatility and low treasury rates make for challenging financial topography. Navigating this financial landscape starts with planful asset management that takes into account your specific needs and options.

Even if you feel that you have plenty of money in your 401(k) or IRA, not knowing how much *risk* those investments are exposed to can cause you major financial suffering. Take the market crash of 2008 for example. In 2008, the average investor lost 30 percent of their 401(k). If more people had shifted their investments away from risk as they neared retirement age (i.e. the Rule of 100), they may have lost a lot less money going into retirement.

When using the Rule of 100 to calculate your level of risk, your financial age might be different than your chronological age, however. The way you organize your assets depends on your goals and your level of comfort with risk. Whatever you determine the appropriate amount of risk for you to be, you will need to organize your portfolio to reflect your goals. If you have more Hope So Money than Know So Money, in particular, you will need to make decisions about how to move it. You can work with a financial professional to find appropriate Know So Money options for your situation.

But how to you arrive at the right ratio of Hope So and Know So money in order to produce both kinds of money: Live On and Leave On? How do you find the right balance between risk and growth for the long term?

Investing heavily in Hope So investments and gambling all of your assets on the market is incredibly risky no matter where you fall within the Rule of 100. Money in the market can't be depended on to generate income, and a plan that leans too heavily on Hope So Money can easily fail, especially when investment decisions are influenced by emotional reactions to market downturns and recoveries. Not only is this an unwise plan, it can be incredibly stressful to an investor who is gambling everything on stocks and mutual funds.

But a plan that uses too much Know So Money avoids all volatility and can also fail. Why? Investing all of your money in Certificates of Deposit (CDs), savings accounts, money markets and other low return accounts may provide interest and income, but that likely won't be enough to keep pace with inflation. If you focus exclusively on income from Know So Money and avoid owning any stocks or mutual funds in your portfolio, you won't be able to leverage the potential for long-term growth your portfolio needs to stay healthy and productive. This is where the Rule of 100 can help you determine how much of your money should be invested in the market to anticipate your future needs.

THE NUMBERS DON'T LIE

When the rubber meets the road, the numbers dictate your options. Your risk tolerance is an important indicator of what kinds of investments you should consider, but if the returns from those investments don't meet your retirement goals, your income needs will likely not be met. For example, if the level of risk you are comfortable with manages your investments at a 4 percent return and you need to realize an 8 percent return, your income needs aren't going to be met when you need to rely on your investments for retirement income. A professional may encourage you to be more aggressive with your investment strategy by taking on more risk in order to give you the potential of earning a greater return. If taking more risk isn't an option that you are comfortable with, then the discussion will turn to how you can earn more money or spend less in order to align your needs with your resources more closely.

How are you going to structure your income flow during retirement? The answer to this question dictates how you determine your risk tolerance. If the numbers say that you need to be more aggressive with your investing, or that you need to modify your lifestyle, it becomes a choice you need to make.

THE RULES OF ENGAGEMENT

Working with a financial professional means working with someone who is focused on your needs, your risk tolerance and your long term plan. An independent financial professional is legally obligated to help you make financial decisions that are in your best interest and fall within your comfort zone. Taking steps toward creating a retirement plan is nothing to take lightly. What is your lifestyle today? Would you like to maintain it into retirement? Are you meeting your needs? Are you happy with your lifestyle? What do you really *need* to live on when you retire?

Some people will have the luxury of maintaining or improving their lifestyle, while others may have to make decisions about what they need versus what they want during their retirement.

Organizing your assets, understanding your investments, and creating an income and accumulation plan for retirement can quickly become an overwhelming task. The fact of the matter is that financial professionals build their careers around understanding the different variables affecting retirement financing.

By leveraging tax strategies, properly organizing your assets, and accumulating helpful financial products that help you meet your income and accumulation needs, you are more likely to meet your goals. You might have a million dollars socked away in a savings account, but your neighbor who has $300,000 in a diverse investment portfolio that takes into account safe and hybrid investments tailored to their needs, may end up enjoying a better retirement lifestyle. Why? They had more than a good work ethic and a penchant for saving. They had the right approach to retirement planning.

CHAPTER 2 RECAP //

- Due to increased longevity and stock market volatility, one of the biggest dilemmas retirees face today is structuring their investments to meet their short-term and long-term income needs. Estate planning is for anybody with an amount of money to manage during retirement.

- In order to maintain your current lifestyle, your retirement savings should be invested in financial tools that provide the right balance between risk, safety and growth.

- There are two types of Know So Money: Live On and Leave On money. It is important to structure your investments to provide you with income for both now and later. Later income can provide you with an increased income to help you pay for long term care; it can also be structured to provide a legacy for your loved ones.

- Understanding where and how your assets are invested is key to the safety of your retirement income. Multiple retirement accounts can create confusion about risk, tax implications, and safety. Taking control of your assets begins with determining your exposure to risk.

- When working with a financial professional, the rules of engagement dictate that they should be focused on your needs/goals/risk tolerance first before trying to sell you any product. They can also help you compose a clear and concise inventory of your assets, and learn how much they are worth, what rules apply to them, and how they are structured for risk.

3

Plan for the Risks & Prepare for the Realities

"Will we outlive our money?"

Jack Hart was a 60 year old who came to see his financial professional two years before retiring. Jack was an avid golfer who liked to fish on the weekends and was in excellent health. He sat down with his financial professional, and they talked about structuring his assets in a way that would provide an income for him during retirement. Jack wanted to continue doing all the things he was used to doing – golfing, fishing, and taking trips to Illinois where his son lived with his wife and their two boys.

The financial professional asked him, "Do you have a strategy in place for long term care? Any long term care insurance or life insurance with a long term care benefit?"

Mr. Hart shook his head, "Nah," he said, "I don't want to think about that stuff now. Why would I need to worry about that? Look at me. I'm in my prime!" And it was true: Jack was a tanned and fit vital-looking 60-year old man. He had saved half a million dollars in assets and had other things on his mind. The financial planner pressed on, "You're doing great now. But what about five or 10 or 15 years down the road? It might be something you want to think about considering you don't have family nearby." But Jack waived the concern away, put it off, and focused on other things instead.

Jack Hart was only 63 when he had a major stroke while out on the golf course. The stroke almost crippled him and he spent months in physical therapy. He had to use a walker to get to and from his car; he had to give up playing golf. After a few years of that, his condition deteriorated and he could no longer fend for himself. His son living in Illinois was busy raising his young family, and Jack's wife had died years ago. Jack needed aid and the attendance of another person on a regular basis and so he had to go to nursing home at age 68. By the time Jack Hart turned 80, every last penny of his half a million dollars was used up. He never saw that stroke coming, and now, he is never coming out of that nursing home. After all his years of hard work and saving, Jack will have no assets to pass on to his son or grandsons.

The cost of long term care is one of the realities of retirement planning that nobody wants to talk about. People like Jack Hart simply think it won't happen to them, and then when it does, the effects are devastating. Had Jack planned for the realities of longevity and the fact, however cruel, that our bodies don't always keep up with us as well as we'd like, his financial professional could have gotten him an annuity with a long term care rider, or an Indexed Universal Life Insurance policy with an income doubler. These are just some of the financial tools that are available to help you plan and prepare for both the risks and realities of life during the retirement years.

THE SIX FACTORS IMPACTING YOUR RETIREMENT

There are several hurdles specific to your retirement years. Preparing for these hurdles will greatly increase the chances that you soar through unscathed. Not only do you need to secure your assets and coordinate an income that you can rely on, you also need to consider the following six factors that can have a major impact on you during your retirement years.

Factor #1: Longevity: Thanks to a healthier lifestyle and medical advances, most seniors today are living longer and stronger into their retirement years. Not only are we living longer, but our life expectancy actually increases the older we get. According to the Society of Actuaries 2000 Mortality Table, a couple that makes it to age 65 has a 99-percent chance of living into their 70s, and 94 percent chance of living into their 80s. That means you need to plan for the realities of what your needs may be at that point in your life.

Factor #2: Inflation: Year in and year out, inflation erodes the purchasing power of your retirement savings. $1,000 saved today and adjusted for inflation (assuming a 4 percent annual rate of inflation) will amount to only $822 in 5 years, and a mere $675 in 10 years.

Factor #3: Taxes: There are a number of strategies that can help you minimize the effect of taxes or even avoid some taxes altogether. The first step will be to review your previous year's tax return with an eye for missed deductions. The Internal Revenue Service tax code has grown to 71,000 pages as of 2010, making working with a tax professional an invaluable tool to ensure you don't pay more taxes than you have to. A $100,000 certificate of deposit kept at a bank that earns 2 percent interest annually actually only gains 1.44 percent net interest after taxes.

Factor #4: Health Care: The rising costs of health care and long term care can quickly drain your retirement savings if not planned for properly. According to Genworth Financial's 2010 Cost of Care Survey, your health care expenses as a retiree could exceed $400,000 over the course of 20 years. When you consider your chances of living another 20 years, it makes sense to create a plan that considers this reality.

Factor #5: Your Asset Allocation: As discussed earlier, proper asset allocation becomes increasingly important as you approach your retirement years. In today's economic climate, it's not enough to have retirement savings – you must have a properly allocated portfolio that can keep up with inflation and protect you against risk. Understanding the fee structure of your investments and exactly what percentage of your money is invested where is key to reducing risk and keeping more of your retirement dollars intact

Factor #6: The Annual return on Your Assets: You don't control the annual return on your assets, but you do control where those assets are invested. As we talked about in the introduction, the math established by the sequence of returns shows us that losing money during the first few years of retirement can significantly impact the odds of outliving your money. The Rule of 72 is a formula discovered by Albert Einstein that states the following: if you can earn 7.2 percent interest per year and not lose any money on your principal, then that money will double every 10 years.

What will you be doing during your retirement years? Moving to a new home? Pursuing a new endeavor? Helping a loved one achieve their goals? Preparing for all the risks and realities that come with the challenges of retiring today will help you lay the ground work for the living roadmap that can take you to the destination of your retirement dreams.

TAKING A CLOSER LOOK AT YOUR ASSETS

Think about your investment portfolio. Think specifically about those investments you've identified as Hope So Money. Do you know what percentage of your portfolio is allocated to Hope So Money, and what percentage is allocated to Know So investment vehicles? You may have several different investment products such as individual mutual funds, bond accounts, stocks, etc. You may have inherited a stock portfolio from a relative, or you might be invested in a bond account offered by the company for which you worked due to your familiarity with them. While you may or may not be managing your investments individually, the reality is that you probably don't have an overall asset allocation strategy for all of your investments. While you may want to have a portion of your investments in Hope So Money vehicles – either for use as Live On or Leave On money – assets that aren't properly allocated with a purpose can unduly expose your retirement savings to risk.

Harnessing the earning potential of your Leave On Money relies on more than a collection of stocks and bonds. When you sit down with an investment professional, you can look at all of your assets together. Chances are that you have accumulated a number of different assets over the last 20, 30 or 50 years. You may have a 401(k), an IRA, a Roth IRA, an account of self-directed stocks, a brokerage account, etc. Wherever you put your money, a financial professional will go through your assets and help you determine the level of risk to which you are exposed now and should be exposed in the future.

Here is a typical example of how an investment professional can be helpful to a future retiree:

» *Stephanie is 65 years old and wants to retire in two years. She has a 401(k) from her job to which she has contributed for 26 years. She also has some stocks that her late husband managed. Stephanie also has $55,000 in a mutual fund that her brother recommended to her five years ago and $30,000 in another mutual fund that she heard about at work. She takes a look at her assets one day and decides that she doesn't understand what they add up to or what kind of retirement they will provide. She decides to meet with an investment professional.*

Stephanie's professional immediately asks her:

Does she know exactly where all of her money is? *Stephanie doesn't know much about all of her husband's stocks, which have now become hers. Their value is at $100,000 invested in three large cap companies. Stephanie is unsure of the companies and whether she should hold or sell them.*

Does she know what types of assets she owns? *Yes and no. She knows she has a 401(k) and an IRA, but she is unfamiliar with her husband's self-directed stock portfolio or the type of mutual funds she owns. Furthermore she is unclear as to how to manage the holdings as she nears retirement.*

Does she know the strategies behind each one of the investment products she owns? *While Stephanie knows she has a 401(k), an IRA and mutual fund holdings, she doesn't know how her 401(k) is organized or how to make it more conservative as she nears retirement. She is unsure whether her IRA is a Roth or traditional variety and how to draw income from them. She really does not have specific investment principles guiding her investment decisions, and she doesn't know anything about her husband's individual stocks. One major concern for Stephanie is whether her family would be okay if she were not around.*

After determining Stephanie's assets, her financial professional prepares a consolidated report that lays out all of her assets for her to review. Her professional explains each one of them to her. Stephanie discovers that although she is two years away from retiring, her 401(k) is organized with an amount of risk with which she is not comfortable. Sixty percent of her 401(k) is at risk, far off the mark if we abide by the Rule of 100. Stephanie opts to be more conservative than the Rule of 100 suggests, as she will rely on her 401(k) for most of her immediate income needs after retirement. Stephanie's professional also points out several instances of overlap between her mutual funds. Stephanie learns that while she is comfortable with one of her mutual funds, she does not agree with the management principles of the other. In the end, Stephanie's professional helps her re-organize her 401(k) to secure her more Know So Money for retirement income. Her professional also uses her mutual fund and her husband's stock assets to create a growth oriented investment plan for Leave On Money that Stephanie will rely on in 15 years when she plans on relocating closer to her children and grandchildren. By creating an overall investment strategy, Stephanie is able to meet her targeted goals in retirement. Stephanie's financial professional worked closely with her and her tax professional to minimize the tax impact of any asset sales on Stephanie's situation.

Like Stephanie, you may have several savings vehicles: a 401(k), an IRA to which you regularly contribute, some mutual funds to which you make monthly contributions, etc. But what is your ***overall investment strategy***? Do you have one in place? Do you want one that will help you meet your retirement goals?

RETIREMENT PLANNING AND THE THREE BEARS

Of the six factors that impact your retirement, there are three bears that most people tend to ignore. As mentioned in the introduction, failing to plan for these three bears can really do a lot of damage. The reasons for ignoring these bears range the gambit from being too complicated to handle alone – such as the bear of taxes – or being in denial that the problem exists – such as the bear of healthcare. Take the time now to look each bear in the eye and make sure they don't disrupt a retirement plan that otherwise would be *just right*.

Bear #1: Taxes.

Perhaps the most impactful piece of retirement planning is determining your current and future tax liability and developing strategies to minimize the amount of taxes you pay in retirement. Tax planning can have a large impact on the amount of wealth you will be able to transfer to your heirs. Meeting with a financial professional helps to ensure that your retirement plan takes full advantage of available tax credits and deductions to ensure that you and your heirs are maximizing wealth for generations to come.

Retirement Strategies & Solutions has a strategic alliance with Stovall and Associates, Ltd; utilizing their team of CPAs to provide tax planning, preparation and filing services for our clients. Our clients receive proactive advice on tax reduction strategies based on income, expenses, individual needs, and goals. Proactive tax planning also allows our clients the opportunity to minimize tax burdens and build a solid foundation of tax reduction strategies that can result in years of tax savings.

Bear #2: Inflation.

Chances are that you will need more money in 20 years to buy the exact same things that you buy today. Inflation does ebb and flow, but it can also quickly erode your retirement savings if not addressed during the income planning stage. Regular raises to your income plan can help counter inflation costs.

According to the 2010 Bureau of Labor Statistics, a dozen eggs cost $.93 in 1989 and $1.50 in 2010. A new car in 1989 averaged $16,000 as compared to $26,000 in 2010. How much will the eggs and the new car cost during your retirement? The performance of your retirement investments is more important now than it ever was, which makes diversification key to sustaining your portfolio for the long haul.

Bear #3: The expense of health care.

According to a 2010 Gallup poll, 76 percent of Americans don't believe they will ever need long term care. This is in line with the way Jack Hart felt, but unfortunately, it's not in line with reality. The Government Accountability Office (GOA) in May of 2008 reported that married couples over the age of 65 have an 80 percent chance that at least one of them will at some time require a nursing home or long term care. Most people have their head in the sand when it comes to this issue. You don't want to fathom the concept and so you stay in denial about the responsibility of funding long term care. It's human nature not to be proactive. We react *after* something bad happens. However, as illustrated by the story of Jack Hart, after is often too late.

Most people make the mistake of thinking they have to be sick in order to need long term care. That's not always the case. As we age, it becomes increasingly difficult to perform simple daily tasks. Menial custodial chores such as taking out the garbage, shopping for food, and other necessities can get harder to do, especially when living alone. Custodial Service is one kind of Home Care available that has nothing to do with your medical condition. A person hired for this type of home care performs activities such as driving, picking up prescriptions, and shopping for groceries; they can also assist with bathing, cooking, and housekeeping.

Home *Health* Care providers, on the other hand, are qualified to dispense medical care and advice. A nursing home in the Dallas Fort Worth area can cost as much as $5,400 a month. While this may be an unpleasant subject to think about, without planning, it's quite possible that today's retirees could lose more of their retirement savings due to the costs of long term care than even the harshest of stock market downturns.

YOUR LIVING ROADMAP

Creating a retirement plan *before* you retire allows you to satisfy your need for lifetime income and address all six factors the impact a healthy retirement. Paying special attention to the three bears will also keep you ahead of the curve. Addressing each of the bears gives more security to your Leave On Money and will potentially allow you to build your legacy down the road.

Here is a basic roadmap of what we have covered so far in the book:

- Sit down with your spouse or loved one and have *the retirement talk*. Address non-monetary issues such as, where do you want to live? And, what would you like to do with your time?
- Review your income needs and look specifically at essential and discretionary expenses. Take control of your assets and determine the amount of risk associated with each asset in terms of Know So Money and Hope So Money.
- Ask yourself where you are in your preservation phase. Is retirement one year away? 10 years away? Last year? Determine how much money you need to Live On and how you need to structure your existing assets to provide for that need as well as money you will need later, known as Leave On Money.
- Address retirement issues that you may find uncomfortable, such as paying taxes and the funding long term care.

CHAPTER 3 RECAP //

- Planning right means taking into consideration the six biggest factors that affect your retirement savings: longevity, inflation, taxes, health care, the allocation of your assets and the return on your assets.
- Taking control of your assets also means answering the questions: *Do you know where your money is? Do you know what type of assets you own? Do you know the strategies behind your investment products?*
- The three bears of retirement are taxes, inflation and the expense of healthcare. It pays to look at those bears today, regardless of how unpleasant it may be. Identifying and implementing solutions today will ensure those bears don't do damage to your retirement savings down the road.

4

An Understanding of Social Security

"Does it matter when I take my Social Security benefit?"

One kind of Know So Money that most Americans can rely on for income when they retire is Social Security. If you're like most Americans, Social Security is or will be an important part of your retirement income and one that you should know how to properly manage. As a first step in creating your income plan, a financial professional will take a look at your Social Security benefit options. Social Security is the foundation of income planning for anyone who is about to retire and is a reliable source of Know So Money in your overall income plan.

Most retirees imagine triggering their Social Security benefits at one of three ages: 62 (earliest eligible Age), 66 (Full Retirement Age), and 70 (age at which monthly maximum benefit is reached.) Unfortunately, in nearly every circumstance, none of these three ages will actually get them their maximum lifetime benefit. Instead, your maximum lifetime benefit is found by running over 20,000 calculations and exploring advanced strategies such as Restricted Application and File and Suspend. Your customized Social Security Maximization report will let you know EXACTLY when and how to file for benefits in order to achieve your maximum lifetime income.

> *Peter is 66 and his wife, Louise is 64. After meeting with their financial planner, they came up with a plan to maximize their lifetime Social Security benefits by utilizing the File and Suspend strategy available to married couples. Louise files for a spousal benefit once she reaches her Full Retirement Age (FRA.) That amount is half of what her husband, Peter's Primary Insurance Amount (PIA) will be. Peter, for his part, chooses to "roll up" his benefit and allows it to continue growing. When Peter reaches age 70, his Social Security is fully ripe and it is only then that Peter begins receiving his benefits. When Louise reaches age 70, she can also max out her Social Security benefit, or she can choose to stay on the spousal benefit. Louise will choose whichever amount is higher.*

There are a lot of terms and phrases associated with Social Security benefits such as FRAs, PIAs and "roll up." Educating yourself about what these terms mean with regards to your Social Security benefits can help you retire right by maximizing your benefit amount. In the scenario above, if Peter and Louise were to simple file at age 62 and begin taking their Social Security benefits, they would earn $682,000 from Social Security benefits by the age of 85.

By exercising their Spousal Planning Option, however, Peter and Louise will earn a total of $882,818 from Social Security by the age of 85. That is a difference of $200,818.

Social Security provides a lifetime benefit in the form of a monthly check that is adjusted each year for inflation to individuals who meet three requirements:
- Must be over age 62.
- Forty credits for covered work, generally satisfied by working at least 10 years in which you had substantial earnings that were subject to Social Security tax or self-employment tax.
- Must apply for the benefit by application.

Here are some facts that illustrate how Social Security works:
- When you receive a paycheck from your employer, you pay into Social Security.
- 6.2 percent of your salary is paid by you and 6.2 percent is paid by your employer.
- Forty credits are needed to be eligible to receive benefits.
- One credit for every $1,160 made annually as of 2013. This amount is indexed each year.
- Maximum four credits per year.
- 2013 average Social Security benefit is $1,261.
- Maximum benefit for 2013 is $2,533.
- Highest 35 years of earnings are used to determine your Social Security benefit.
- If you work less than 35 years, the missing years are counted as zero.
- Maximum taxable income is $113,700.*

---

*http://www.aarp.org/work/social-security/question-and-answer1/info-2014/how-it-works-social-security-q-and-a-tool-category.html

Here are some facts that illustrate how Americans currently use Social Security:

- 90 percent of Americans age 65 and older receive Social Security benefits.*
- Social Security provides 39 percent of income for retired Americans.*
- Claiming Social Security benefits at the wrong time can reduce your monthly benefit by up to 57 percent.**
- 43 percent of men and 48 percent of women claim Social Security benefits at age 62.**
- 74 percent of retirees receive reduced Social Security benefits.**
- In 2013, the average monthly Social Security benefit was $1,261. The maximum benefit for 2013 was $2,533.
- The $1,272 monthly benefit reduction between the average and the maximum is applied for life.***

It is important to note that Social Security income is subject to taxes.

HOW SOCIAL SECURITY WORKS

There are many aspects of Social Security that are well known and others that aren't. When it comes time for you to cash in on your Social Security benefit, you will have many options and choices. Social Security is a massive government program that manages retirement benefits for millions of people. Experts spend their entire careers understanding and analyzing it. Luckily, you don't have to understand all of the intricacies of Social Security to

---

*http://www.ssa.gov/pressoffice/basicfact.htm

**When to Claim Social Security Benefits, David Blanchett, CFA, CFP® January, 2013

***http://www.socialsecurity.gov/pressoffice/factsheets/colafacts2013.com

maximize its advantages. You simply need to know the best way to manage your Social Security benefit. You need to know exactly what to do to get the most from your Social Security benefit and when to do it. Taking the time to create a roadmap for your Social Security strategy will help ensure that you are able to exact your maximum benefit and efficiently coordinate it with the rest of your retirement plan.

There are many aspects of Social Security that you have no control over. You don't control how much you put into it, and you don't control what it's invested in or how the government manages it. However, you do control when and how you file for benefits. The real question about Social Security that you need to answer is, "When should I start taking Social Security?" While this is the all-important question, there are a couple of key pieces of information you need to track down first.

Before we get into a few calculations and strategies that can make all the difference, let's start by covering the basic information about Social Security which should give you an idea of where you stand. Just as the foundation of a house creates the stable platform for the rest of the framework to rest upon, your Social Security benefit is an important part of your overall retirement plan. The purpose of the information that follows is not to give an exhaustive explanation of how Social Security works, but to give you some tools and questions to start understanding how Social Security affects your retirement and how you can prepare for it.

Let's start with eligibility.

Eligibility. Understanding how and when you are eligible for Social Security benefits will help clarify what to expect when the time comes to claim them.

To receive retirement benefits from Social Security, you must earn eligibility. In almost all cases, Americans born after 1929 must earn 40 quarters of credit to be eligible to draw their Social

Security retirement benefit. In 2013, a Social Security credit represents $1,160 earned in a calendar quarter. The number changes as it is indexed each year, but not drastically. In 2012, a credit represented $1,130. Four quarters of credit is the maximum number that can be earned each year. In 2013, an American would have had to earn at least $4,640 to accumulate four credits. In order to qualify for retirement benefits, you must have earned a minimum number of credits. Additionally, if you are at least 62 years old and have been married to a recipient of Social Security benefits for at least 12 months, you can choose to receive Spousal Benefits. Although 40 is the minimum number of credits required to begin drawing benefits, it is important to know that once you claim your Social Security benefit, there is no going back. Although there may be cost of living adjustments made, you are locked into that base benefit amount forever.

Primary Insurance Amount. You can think of your Primary Insurance Amount (PIA) like a ripening fruit. It represents the amount of your Social Security benefit at your Full Retirement Age (FRA). Your benefit becomes fully ripe at your FRA, and will neither reduce nor increase due to early or delayed retirement options. If you opt to take benefits before your FRA, however, your monthly benefit will be less than your PIA. You will essentially be picking an unripened fruit. On the one hand, waiting until after your FRA to access your benefits will increase your benefit beyond your PIA. On the other hand, you don't want the fruit to overripen, because every month you wait is one less check you get from the government.

Full Retirement Age. Your FRA is an important figure for anyone who is planning to rely on Social Security benefits in their retirement. Depending on when you were born, there is a specific age at which you will attain FRA. Your FRA is dictated by your year

AN UNDERSTANDING OF SOCIAL SECURITY

of birth and is the age at which you can begin your full monthly benefit. Your FRA is important because it is half of the equation used to calculate your Social Security benefit. The other half of the equation is based on when you start taking benefits.

When Social Security was initially set up, the FRA was age 65, and it still is for people born before 1938. But as time has passed, the age for receiving full retirement benefits has increased. If you were born between 1938 and 1960, your full retirement age is somewhere on a sliding scale between 65 and 67. Anyone born in 1960 or later will now have to wait until age 67 for full benefits. Increasing the FRA has helped the government reduce the cost of the Social Security program, which pays out more than a half trillion dollars to beneficiaries every year!*

While you can begin collecting benefits as early as age 62, the amount you receive as a monthly benefit will be less than it would be if you wait until you reached your FRA or surpass your FRA. It is important to note that if you file for Social Security benefit before your FRA, *the reduction to your monthly benefit will remain in place for the rest of your life.* You can also delay receiving benefits up to age 70, in which case your benefits will be higher than your PIA for the rest of your life.

- At FRA, 100 percent of PIA is available as a monthly benefit.
- At age 62, your Social Security retirement benefits are available. For each month you take benefits prior to your FRA, however, the monthly amount of your benefit is reduced. *This reduction stays in place for the rest of your life.*
- At age 70, your monthly benefit reaches its maximum. After you turn age 70, your monthly benefit will no longer increase.

---

*http://www.ssa.gov/pressoffice/basicfact.htm

Year of Birth	Full Retirement Age
1943-1954	66
1955	66 and 2 months
1956	66 and 4 months
1957	66 and 6 months
1958	66 and 8 months
1959	66 and 10 months
1960 or later	age 67*

ROLLING UP YOUR SOCIAL SECURITY

Your Social Security income "rolls up" the longer you wait to claim it. Your monthly benefit will continue to increase until you turn 70 years old. But because Social Security is the foundation of most people's retirement, many Americans feel that they don't have control over how or when they receive their benefits. As a matter of fact, only 4 percent of Americans wait until after their FRA to file for benefits! This trend persists, despite the fact that every dollar you increase your Social Security income by means less money you will have to spend from your nest egg to meet your retirement income needs! For many people, creating their Social Security strategy is the most important decision they can make to positively impact their retirement. *The difference between the best and worst Social Security decision can be tens of thousands of dollars over a lifetime of benefits — up to $170,000!*

Deciding NOW or LATER: Following the above logic, it makes sense to wait as long as you can to begin receiving your Social Security benefit. However, the answer isn't always that simple. Not everyone has the option of waiting. Many people need to rely on Social Security on day one of their retirement. In fact, *nearly 50 percent of 62-year-old Americans file for Social Secu-*

**http://www.ssa.gov/OACT/progdata/nra.html*

rity benefits. Why is this number so high? Some might need the income. Others might be in poor health and don't feel they will live long enough to make FRA worthwhile for themselves or their families. It is also possible, however, that the majority of folks taking an early benefit at age 62 are simply under-informed about Social Security. Perhaps they make this major decision based on rumors and emotion.

File Immediately if You:
Find your job is unbearable.
Are willing to sacrifice retirement income.
Are not healthy and need a reliable source of income.

Consider Delaying Your Benefit if You:
Want to maximize your retirement income.
Want to increase retirement benefits for your spouse.
Are still working and like it.
Are healthy and willing / able to wait to file.

So if you decide to wait, how long should you wait? Lots of people can put it off for a few years, but not everyone can wait until they are 70 years old. Your individual circumstances may be able to help you determine when you should begin taking Social Security. If you do the math, you will quickly see that between ages 62 and 70, there are 96 months in which you can file for your Social Security benefit. If you take into account those 96 months and the 96 months your spouse could also file for Social Security, the number of different strategies for structuring your benefit, you can easily end up with more than 20,000 different scenarios. It's safe to say this isn't the kind of math that most people can easily handle. Each month would result in a different benefit amount. The longer you wait, the higher your monthly benefit amount becomes. Each month you wait, however, is one less month that you receive a Social Security check.

The goal is to maximize your lifetime benefits. That may not always mean waiting until you can get the largest monthly payment. Taking the bigger picture into account, you want to find out how to get the most money out of Social Security over the number of years that you draw from it. Don't underestimate the power of optimizing your benefit: the difference between the BEST and WORST Social Security election can easily be between $30,000 to $50,000 in lifetime benefits. *The difference can be very substantial!*

If you know that every month you wait, your Social Security benefit goes up a little bit, and you also know that every month you wait, you receive one less benefit check, how do you determine where the sweet spot is that maximizes your benefits over your lifetime? Financial professionals have access to software that will calculate the best year and month for you to file for benefits based on your default life expectancy. You can further customize that information by estimating your life expectancy based on your health, habits and family history. If you can then create an income plan (we'll get into this later in the chapter) that helps you wait until the target date for you to file for Social Security, you can optimize your retirement income strategy to get the most out of your Social Security benefit. How can you calculate your life expectancy? Well, you don't know exactly how long you'll live, but you have a better idea than the government does. They rely on averages to make their calculations. *You have much more personal information about your health, lifestyle and family history than they do.* You can use that knowledge to game the system and beat all the other people who are making uninformed decisions by filing early for Social Security.

While you can and should educate yourself about how Social Security works, the reality is you don't need to know a lot of general information about Social Security in order to make choices about your retirement. What you do need to know is exactly ***what to do to maximize your benefit***. Because knowing what you need to do has huge impacts on your retirement! For most Americans, Social Security is the foundation of income planning for retirement. Social Security benefits represent nearly 40 percent of the income of retirees.* For many people, it can represent the largest portion of their retirement income. Not treating your Social Security benefit as an asset and investment tool can lead to sub-optimization of your largest source of retirement income.

Let's take a look at an example that shows the impact of working with a financial professional to optimize Social Security benefits:

> » *Bob and Viv Danbury are a typical American couple who have worked their whole lives and saved when they could. Bob is 60 years old, and Viv is 56 years old. They sat down with a financial professional who logged onto the Social Security website to look up their PIAs. Bob's PIA is $1,900 and Viv's is $900.*
>
> *If the Danburys cash in at age 62 and begin taking retirement benefits from Social Security, they will receive an estimated $492,000 in lifetime benefits. That may seem like a lot, but if you divide that amount over 20 years, it averages out to be just shy of $25,000 per year. The Danburys are accustomed to a more significant annual income than that. To make up the difference, they will have to rely on alternative retirement income options. They will basically have to depend on a bigger nest egg to provide them with the income they need.*
>
> *If they wait until their FRA, they will increase their lifetime benefits to an estimated $523,700. This option allows*

---

*http://www.ssa.gov/pressoffice/basicfact.htm

them to achieve their Primary Insurance Amount, which will provide them a $33,000 annual income.

After learning the Danburys' needs and using software to calculate the most optimal time to begin drawing benefits, the Danburys' financial professional determined that the best option for them drastically increases their potential lifetime benefits to $660,000!

By using strategies that their financial professional recommended, they increased their potential lifetime benefits by as much as **$148,000.** *There's no telling how much you could miss out on from your Social Security if you don't take time to create a strategy that calculates your maximum benefit. For the Danburys, the value of maximizing their benefits was the difference between night and day. While this may seem like a special case, it isn't uncommon to find benefit increases of this magnitude. You'll never know unless you take a look at your own options.*

Despite the importance of knowing when and how to take your Social Security benefit, many of today's retirees and pre-retirees may know little about the mechanics of Social Security and how they can maximize their benefit.

So, to whom should you turn for advice when making this complex decision? Before you pick up the phone and call Uncle Sam, you should know that the Social Security Administration (SSA) representatives are actually prohibited from giving you election advice! Plus, SSA representatives in general are trained to focus on monthly benefit amounts, not the lifetime income for a family.

MAXIMIZING YOUR LIFETIME BENEFIT

Calculating how to maximize lifetime benefits is more important than waiting until age 70 for your maximum monthly benefit amount. It's about getting the most income during your lifetime. Professional benefit maximization software can target the year and month that it is most beneficial for you to file based on your life expectancy.

Remember, every month you wait to file, the amount of your benefit check goes up, but you also get one less check. You don't know how exactly how long you're going to live, but you have a better idea of your life expectancy than the actuaries at the Social Security Administration who can only work with averages. They can't make calculations based on your specific situation. A professional can run the numbers for you and get the target date that maximizes your potential lifetime benefits. You can't get this information from the SSA, but you *can* get it from a financial professional.

Your Social Security options don't stop here, however. There are a plethora of other choices you can make to manipulate your benefit payments.

Social Security Benefits For Married Couples:
- File and Suspend: As demonstrated by our story at the beginning of the chapter, this concept allows for a lower-earning spouse to receive up to 50 percent of the other's PIA amount if both spouses file for benefits at the right time.
- Restricted Application: A higher-earning spouse may be able to start collecting a spousal benefit on the lower-earning spouse's benefit while allowing his or her benefit to continue to grow. Be clear when you file that you are restricting the application to the spousal benefit only, and not collecting your own benefit. This strategy can help maximize your overall lifetime family benefit, but may not result in the highest individual monthly benefit.

- Spousal Benefit. The Spousal Benefit is available to the spouse of someone who is eligible for Retired Worker Benefits. What if there was a way for your spouse to receive his or her benefit for four years and not lose the chance to get his or her maximum benefit when he or she turns age 70? Many people do not know about this strategy and might be missing out on benefits they have earned.
- Survivorship Benefit. When one spouse passes away, the survivor is able to receive the larger of the two benefit amounts.

THE DIVORCE FACTOR

How does a divorced spouse qualify for benefits? If you have gone through a divorce, it might affect the retirement benefit to which you are entitled.

A person can receive benefits as a divorced spouse on a former spouse's Social Security record if he or she:

- Was married to the former spouse for at least 10 years;
- Is at least age 62 years old;
- Is unmarried; and
- Is not entitled to a higher Social Security benefit on his or her own record.*

With all of the different options, strategies and benefits to choose from, you can see why filing for Social Security is more complicated than just mailing in the paperwork. Gathering the data and making yourself aware of all your different options isn't enough to know exactly what to do, however. On the one hand, you can knock yourself out trying to figure out which options are best for you and wondering if you made the best decision. On the other hand, you can work with a financial professional who uses

SSA.gov

customized software that takes all the variables of your specific situation into account and calculates your best option. You have tens of thousands of different options for filing for your Social Security benefit. If your spouse is a different age than you are, it nearly doubles the amount of options you have. This is far more complicated arithmetic than most people can do on their own. If you want a truly accurate understanding of when and how to file, you need someone who will ask you the right questions about your situation, someone who has access to specialized software that can crunch the numbers. The reality is that you need to work with a professional that can provide you with the sophisticated analysis of your situation that will help you make a truly informed decision.

Important Questions about Your Social Security Benefit:

- How can I maximize my lifetime benefit? By knowing when and how to file for Social Security. This usually means waiting until you have at least reached your Full Retirement Age. A professional has the experience and the tools to help determine when and how you can maximize your lifetime benefits.
- Who will provide reliable advice for making these decisions? Only a professional has the tools and experience to provide you reliable advice.
- Will the Social Security Administration provide me with the advice? The Social Security Administration cannot provide you with advice or strategies for claiming your benefit. They can give you information about your monthly benefit, but that's it. They also don't have the tools to tell you what your specific best option is. They can accurately answer how the system works, but they can't advise you on what decision to make as to how and when to file for benefits.

The Maximization Report that your financial professional will generate represents an invaluable resource for understanding how and when to file for your Social Security benefit. When you get your customized Social Security Maximization Report, you will not only know all the options available to you – but you will understand the financial implications of each choice. In addition to the analysis, you will also get a report that shows *exactly* at what age – including which month and year – you should trigger benefits and how you should apply. It also includes a variety of other time-specific recommendations, such as when to apply for Medicare or take Required Minimum Distributions from your qualified plans. A report means there is no need to wonder, or to try to figure out when to take action – the Social Security Maximization Report lays it all out for you in plain English.

CHAPTER 4 RECAP //

- Deciding when to take your Social Security benefit is one of the most important decisions you make as a retiree. After the first year of taking the benefit, that amount is locked in for the duration of your lifetime.
- Social Security is a massive, government-funded program and there are many things about this program that you cannot control. You can, however, control when and how you file for benefits.
- To get the most out of your Social Security benefit, you need to file at the right time.
- An Investment Advisor can help you determine when you should file for Social Security to get your Maximum Lifetime Benefit.
- Remember that Social Security benefits are subject to income taxes. (See Chapter 8)

5

What Goes Up Must Come Down

THE STOCK MARKET AND YOUR MONEY

"Should I stay or should I go?"

Debbie worked for a restaurant supply and distribution company for 34 years. During her time there, she received bonuses and pay raises that often included shares of stock in the company. She also dedicated part of her paycheck every month to a 401(k) that bought stock in the company. By the time she retired, Debbie had $250,000 worth of company stock.

Although she had contributed to her 401(k) account every month, Debbie didn't cultivate any other assets that could generate income for her during retirement. Debbie also retired early at age 62 because of her failing health. The commute to work every day was becoming difficult in her weakened condition and she wanted to enjoy the rest of her life in retirement instead of working in the cramped office of the restaurant supply company.

Because she retired early, Debbie failed to maximize her Social Security benefit. While she lives a modest lifestyle, her income needs are $3,500 per month. Debbie's monthly Social Security check only covers $1,900, leaving her with a $1,600 income gap. To supplement her Social Security check, Debbie needs to sell $1,600 of company stock each month to meet her income needs. A $250,000 401(k) is nothing to sneeze at, but reducing its value by $1,600 every month will decimate her savings within 10 years. And that's if the market stays neutral or grows modestly. If the market takes a downturn, the money that Debbie is currently relying on to fill her income gap will rapidly diminish. Even if the market starts going up in a couple of years, it will take much larger gains for her to recover the value that she lost due to the math of rebounds (which will be explained shortly).

Unhappily for Debbie, she retired in 2007, just before the major market downturn that lasted for several years. She lost more than 20 percent of the value of her stock. Because Debbie needed to sell her stock to meet her basic income needs, the market price of the stock was secondary to her need for the money. When she needed money, she was forced to sell however many shares she needed to fill her income gap that month. And if she has a financial crisis, involving a need for long term medical care, for example, she will be forced to sell stock even if the market is low and her shares are worth less. Debbie realizes that she could have relied on an investment structured to deliver her a regular income while protecting the value of her investment. She could have kept her $250,000 from diminishing while enjoying her lifestyle into retirement regardless of the volatility of the market. Ideally, Debbie would have restructured her 401(k) to reflect the level of risk that she was able to take. In her case, she would have had most of her money in a Know So Money assets, allowing her to rely on the value of her assets when she needed them.

It can be challenging to watch the stock market's erratic changes every month, week or even every day. When you have the security of your retirement income riding on it, the ride can feel pretty bumpy. Should you stay in the market and re-grow your assets? Or get out now and move your money to safer investment vehicles? The "*should I stay or should I go*" investment dilemma has never been trickier. History shows us that most market downturns are followed by periods of substantial market increase. Pre and post-retirees with their money in guaranteed products may miss out on opportunities to grow their Leave On money when the market recovers. However, a year after the 2001 recession, the S&P 500 dropped by 12.84 percent.* Keeping your assets solely in equities exposes your Live On Money to the whims and risk of market loss. What's a retiree to do?

EMOTIONS AND MONEY

When you are managing your money by yourself, emotions inevitably enter into the mix. The Dow Jones Industrial Average and the S&P 500 represent more to you than market fluctuations. They represent a portion of your retirement. It's hard not to be emotional about it.

Everyone knows you should buy low and sell high. But what is more likely to happen has been well-documented in the following report:

In 2013, DALBAR, the well-respected financial services market research firm, released their annual "Quantitative Analysis of Investment Behavior" report (QAIB). The report studied the impact of market volatility on individual investors: people like Debbie, or anyone who was managing (or mismanaging) their own investments in the stock market.

National Bureau of Economic Research. Stock market performance based on the Standard and Poor's 500 index.

According to the study, volatility not only caused investors to make decisions based on their emotions, those decisions also harmed their investments and prevented them from realizing potential gains. So why do people meddle so much with their investments when the market is fluctuating? Part of the reason is that many people have financial obligations that they don't have control over. Significant expenses like house payments, the unexpected cost of replacing a broken-down car, and medical bills can put people in a position where they need money. If they need to sell investments to come up with that money, they don't have the luxury of selling when they *want* to. They must sell when they *need* to.

DALBAR's "Quantitative Analysis of Investor Behavior" has been used to measure the effects of investors' buying, selling and mutual fund switching decisions since 1994. The QAIB shows time and time again over nearly a 20 year period that the average investor earns less, and in many cases, significantly less than the performance of mutual funds suggests. QAIB's goal is to improve independent investor performance and to help financial professionals provide helpful advice and investment strategies that address the concerns and behaviors of the average investor.

An excerpt from the report claims that:

"QAIB offers guidance on how and where investor behaviors can be improved. No matter what the state of the mutual fund industry, boom or bust: Investment results are more dependent on investor behavior than on fund performance. Mutual fund investors who hold on to their investments are more successful than those who time the market.

QAIB uses data from the Investment Company Institute (ICI), Standard & Poor's and Barclays Capital Index Products to compare mutual fund investor returns to an appropriate set of benchmarks.

There are actually three primary causes for the chronic shortfall for both equity and fixed income investors:

- *Capital not available to invest. This accounts for 25 percent to 35 percent of the shortfall.*
- *Capital needed for other purposes. This accounts for 35 percent to 45 percent of the shortfall.*
- *Psychological factors. These account for 45 percent to 55 percent of the shortfall."*

The key findings of Dalbar's QAIB report provide compelling statistics about how individual investment strategies produced negative outcomes for the majority of investors:

- Psychological factors account for 45 percent to 55 percent of the chronic investment return shortfall for both equity and fixed income investors.
- Asset allocation is designed to handle the investment decision-making for the investor, which can materially reduce the shortfall due to psychological factors.
- Successful asset allocation investing requires investors to act on two critical imperatives:
- Balance capital preservation and appreciation so that they are aligned with the investor's objective.
- Select a qualified allocator.
- The best way for an investor to determine their risk tolerance is to utilize a risk tolerance assessment. However, these assessments must be accessible and usable.
- Evaluating allocator quality requires analysis of the allocator's underlying investments, decision making process and whether or not past efforts have produced successful outcomes.
- Choosing a top allocator makes a significant difference in the investment results one will achieve.
- Mutual fund retention rates suggest that the average investor has not remained invested for long enough periods to derive the potential benefits of the investment markets.

- Retention rates for asset allocation funds exceed those of equity and fixed income funds by over a year.
- Investors' ability to correctly time the market is highly dependent on the direction of the market. Investors generally guess right more often in up markets. However, in 2012 investors guessed right only 42 percent of the time during a bull market.
- Analysis of investor fund flows compared to market performance further supports the argument that investors are unsuccessful at timing the market. Market upswings rarely coincide with mutual fund inflows while market downturns do not coincide with mutual fund outflows.
- Average equity mutual fund investors gained 15.56 percent compared to a gain of 15.98 percent that just holding the S&P 500 produced.
- The shortfall in the long-term annualized return of the average mutual fund equity investor and the S&P 500 continued to decrease in 2012.
- The fixed-income investor experienced a return of 4.68 percent compared to an advance of 4.21 percent on the Barclays Aggregate Bond Index.
- The average fixed income investor has failed to keep up with inflation in nine out of the last 14 years.*

It doesn't take a financial services market research report to tell you that market volatility is out of your control. The report does prove, however, that before you experience market volatility, you should have an investment plan, and when the market is fluctuating, you should stand by your plan. This harkens back to the story at the beginning of the book, when Mr. and Mrs. Jones were flying an airplane that developed a fuel leak. When the stock

2013 QAIB, Dalbar, March 2013

market takes a downturn, the dollars you've worked so hard to save begin leaking out of your account. It's natural to have an emotional reaction to that, and do one of two things: react like a deer-in-the-headlights and do nothing, keeping everything as is; or, jump ship, leap from the plan, sell your stocks and get out while you can. Having a plan helps to steady the emotions of bad news during turbulent times.

You should review and discuss your investment plan with your financial professional on a regular basis, ensuring he/she is aware of any changes in your goals, financial circumstances, your health or your risk tolerance. When the economy is under stress and the markets are volatile, investors can feel vulnerable. That vulnerability causes people to tinker with their portfolios in an attempt to outsmart the market. Financial professionals, however, don't try to time the market for their clients. They have the ability to remain un-emotional when it comes to your money, and are better able to make decisions based on the numbers, and not those emotions. Using these numbers as their guide, they can tap into the gains that can be realized by committing to long-term investment strategies.

MATH OF REBOUNDS

Taking a hit in the market hurts no matter how stable your income, but most people don't realize that it requires an even larger step forward to return to where you were once you take that step back. You might have the sentiment, "the market always comes back," but even if you do get back to where you were before the loss, your money isn't growing and earning the same way it was before the hit occurred. The math of rebounds, as it is known, uses the percentage of the investment, and not the dollar amount, to calculate what you will need to earn in order to recapture your loses.

For example, if you had $100,000 invested in the stock market in 2007, and along comes the downturn of 2008, the market takes a reduction of 50 percent. So now your $100,000 becomes $50,000. What has to happen for us to get back up to $100,000? It took a 50 percent loss to lose $50,000 but it will take a 100-percent gain to get your account back to where you were before. It takes a LONG time to dig out of the hole.

SEQUENCE OF RETURNS

Whether the market is high or low at the time of your retirement is another thing that's out of your control. This bears mentioning because most people don't realize that it's the *sequence of returns* that influences you're account value even more than the *actual rate of return*. Let's take a look at the following example:

> » *Harold and Irene retired in 1995. They had $500,000 invested in stocks in the S&P 500, and are taking out $25,000, or 5 percent per year, to supplement their retirement income. The value of their account at the end of the year 2013 was $1,200,000. Their neighbors, Fred and Josie are a few years younger, and they retired in the year 2000. They did exactly the same thing as Harold and Irene, withdrawing $25,000 per year from a $500,000 investment held in the stock market. The value of their account at the end of the year 2013 was $94,000.*

This huge discrepancy is due to the sequence of returns. The only thing Fred and Josie did differently was to retire five years later, yet that made a big difference in how their gains were calculated. During the first three years of their retirement, they took three big hits, while in the case of Harold and Irene, those same three big hits were calculated at the end of the 13-year period as opposed to at the beginning. How will your gains be calculated?

Well that all depends on how the market performs, and *the order in which it performs.* You may have the same $500,000 as a starting principal, with an average inflation rate of 3 percent and an average rate of return at 8.43 percent, but it is the sequence of returns that dictates what your final balance will be.

When answering the question, "should I stay or should I go?" during your retirement years, be sure to factor in the math of rebounds and the sequence of returns when making your decision.

SEEKING FINANCIAL ADVICE: STOCK BROKERS VS. INVESTMENT ADVISOR REPRESENTATIVES

As you begin to think about how you should invest your money, there are two basic sources that you've probably considered going to for help: a stock broker or an investment advisor. While either of these financial professionals can help you invest your money in the market, they will most likely do so in very different ways because advice given to you by a stockbroker, or a commission-based registered representative, will probably be quite a bit different than the advice given to you by a fee-based Investment Advisor Representative.

As a result, it's important to understand the difference between the two before you entrust one with your money. A good place to begin is to understand why someone might choose to work with an independent registered investment advisor in the first place. In a survey taken by TD Ameritrade, investors listed the following as the top reasons they selected an independent registered investment advisor:*

- Registered Investment Advisors are required, as fiduciaries, to offer advice that is in the best interest of clients

---

2011 Advisor Sentiment Study, commissioned by TD AMERITRADE. TD Ameritrade, Inc.

- More personalized service and competitive fee structure offered at a Registered Investment Advisor firm
- Dissatisfaction with full commission brokers

The truth is that there is a great deal of difference between stock brokers and investment advisor representatives. For starters, investment advisor representatives are obligated to act in an investor's best interests in every and all aspects of a financial relationship. Confusion continues to exist among investors struggling to find the best financial advice out there and the most credible sources of advice.

Here is some information to help clear up the confusion so you can find good advice from a professional you can trust:

- Investment advisor representatives have the fiduciary duty to act in a client's best interest at all times with every investment decision they make. Stock brokers and brokerage firms usually do not act as fiduciaries to their investors and are not obligated to make decisions that are entirely in the best interest of their customers. For example, if you decide you want to invest in precious metals, a stock broker would offer you a precious metals account from their firm. An Investment Advisor would find you a precious metals account that is the best fit for you based on the investment strategy of your portfolio.
- Investment advisors give their clients a Form ADV describing the methods that the professional uses to do business. An Investment Advisor also obtains client consent regarding any conflicts of interest that could exist with the business of the professional.
- Stock brokers and brokerage firms are not obligated to provide comparable types of disclosure to their customers.
- Whereas stock brokers and firms routinely earn large profits by trading as principal with customers, Investment

Advisors cannot trade with clients as principal (except in very limited and specific circumstances).

- Investment Advisors charge a pre-negotiated fee with their clients in advance of any transactions. They cannot earn additional profits or commissions from their customers' investments without prior consent. Registered Investment Advisors are commonly paid an asset-based fee that aligns their interests with those of their clients. Brokerage firms and stock brokers, on the other hand, have much different payment agreements. Their revenues may increase regardless of the performance of their customers' assets.
- Unlike brokerage firms, where investment banking and underwriting are commonplace, Registered Investment Advisors must manage money in the best interests of their customers. Because Registered Investment Advisors charge set fees for their services, their focus is on their client. Brokerage firms may focus on other aspects of the firm that do not contribute to the improvement of their clients' assets.
- Unlike brokers, Registered Investment Advisors do not get commissions from fund or insurance companies for selling their investment products.

Just to drive home the point, here is what a fiduciary duty to a client means for a Registered Investment Advisor. Registered Investment Advisors must:

- Always act in the best interest of their client and make investment decisions that reflect their goals.
- Identify and monitor securities that are illiquid.
- When appropriate, employ fair market valuation procedures.

- Observe procedures regarding the allocation of investment opportunities, including new issues and the aggregation of orders.
- Have policies regarding affiliated broker-dealers and maintenance of brokerage accounts.
- Disclose all conflicts of interest.
- Have policies on use of brokerage commissions for research.
- Have policies regarding directed brokerage, including step-out trades and payment for order flow.
- Abide by a code of ethics.

When it comes to your stock portfolio, there are clear benefits to working with a Registered Investment Advisor. That said, however, your investment portfolio should only be one component of your retirement plan. Consequently, it's crucial to first find a financial professional who can help you craft an overarching plan for your retirement, and then seek out those financial professionals who can help you hone specific areas of it.

CHAPTER 5 RECAP //
- Emotions inevitably enter the mix during stock market downturns. According to the DALBAR "Quantitative Analysis of Investment Behavior" report released in 2013, the average investor managing their money alone failed to keep up with inflation in nine out of the last 14 years.
- When you take a loss on the stock market, you have to do more than just earn back your initial loss in order to get back to where you were before. The math of rebounds uses the percentage of the investment and not dollar amount to calculate what you need to earn in order to recapture your losses.

- The sequence of returns tells us that in addition to how the market performs, the order of those returns is just as important when it comes to calculating the value of our investments.
- Financial professionals don't try to out-smart the market when managing investments for their clients. Instead, they tap into the potential for gains by committing to proven and long-term investment strategies.
- Investment Advisors are obligated to make investment decisions or recommendations that are in your best interests and are aligned with your financial situation, time frame and risk tolerance, and to put your interests ahead of their own. Stock brokers and brokerage firms are obligated to make suitable recommendations from the universe of products they are permitted to sell.

6

The New Annuities: Today's Do-It-Yourself Pension Plans

"Why hasn't anyone told me about this?"

Joe and Victoria are 62 years old and have decided to run the numbers to see what their retirement is going to look like. They know they currently need $6,000 per month to pay their bills and maintain their current lifestyle. They have also done their Social Security homework and have determined that, between the two of them, they will receive $4,200 per month in benefits. They also receive $350 per month in rent from a tenant who lives in a small carriage house in their backyard. Between their Social Security and the monthly rent income, they will be short $1,450 per month.

They do have an additional asset, however. They have been contributing for years to an IRA that has reached a value of $350,000. They realize that they have to figure out how to turn the $350,000 in their IRA into $1,450 per month for the rest of their life.

At first glance, it may seem like they will have plenty of money. With some quick calculations, they find they have 240 months, or nearly 20 years, of monthly income before they exhaust the account. When you consider income tax, the potential for higher taxes in the future, and market fluctuations (because many IRAs are invested in the market), the amount in the IRA seems to have a little less clout. Every dollar Joe and Victoria take out of the IRA is subject to income tax, and if they leave the remainder in the IRA, they run the risk of losing money in a volatile market. Once they retire and stop getting a paycheck every two weeks, they also stop contributing to their IRA. And when they aren't supplementing its growth with their own money, they are entirely dependent on market growth. That's a scary prospect. They could also withdraw the money from the IRA and put it in a savings account or CD, but removing all the money at once will put them in a tax bracket that will claim a huge portion of the value of the IRA. A seemingly straightforward asset has now become a complicated equation. Joe and Victoria don't know what to do.

After you have calculated your Social Security benefit and have selected the year and month that will maximize your lifetime benefits, it's time to look at your other retirement assets, incomes and options that can fill in your monthly income needs. Like Joe and Victoria, you may have a pension, an IRA or Roth IRA, dividends from stock holdings, money from the sale of real estate, rental property, or other sources of income. But how can these assets be structured so as to provide a protected, guaranteed income stream that grows enough to keep up with inflation and taxes?

You want an investment tool that is *just right*. To use an analogy from the story of Goldilocks and the Three Bears, bank CDs and money market accounts are not generating enough interest to keep up with the combined factors of inflation and taxes. Like the chair in the famous story, they are *too soft*. On the other hand, stocks, bonds and mutual funds have risks attached to them. As discussed in the previous chapter, if you want the market ups, you subject yourself to the market downs, but once you near retirement age, you can't afford those market downturns. These kinds of investments as you near or enter your retirement years are *too hard*.

Is there an investment tool out there that, like the chair in the fairytale, is *just right*? You want the safety of a guaranteed principal, growth that keeps up with inflation, and an income stream you can count on for the rest of your life. Is there a way to achieve this ideal in today's less-than-ideal economy?

HOW TO PROTECT YOUR MONEY IN ANY MARKET

Different financial tools are designed to do different things. Checking and savings accounts provide you with liquid funds to pay the bills; health insurance pays the medical bills; and accounts earmarked for accumulation such as 401(k), 403(b) or IRAs grow your money for your retirement years. Once you begin the transition into your retirement years, you need a financial tool that can protect and grow your money so it can provide an income for you, either now or a few years down the road. There is a financial tool out there designed to create income while providing protection of principal and the potential for growth. This tool is the equity indexed annuity.

Today's new indexed annuities give retirees the best of both worlds: protection and growth. These products are similar to other annuities offered by insurance companies but differ in that they are linked to the stock market in such a way that allows you to capitalize on the earnings without having to take the hits. Unlike a variable annuity that can fluctuate with the market, a Fixed

Indexed Annuity (FIA) **protects** the value of your principal (the full amount that you contribute). FIAs also have built-in safeguards that protect past gains. What you have is a product that offers safety of principal and growth aggressive enough to keep up with inflation. Does this sound too good to be true?

Consider a 2003 published study conducted by the nationally recognized Advantage Group. From September 1998 to September 2003, the stock market experienced both incredible growth and incredible loss. Many retirees lost huge amounts of money during those years, putting the safety of their retirement income at peril. How would their money have done over that same five-year period had it been transferred into an FIA? According to the Advantage Group Research study that examined the performance of the 14 different fixed annuity options available in 1998 (and there are many more available today,) fixed indexed annuities that reset annually averaged a return of more than 7 percent per year even during the steep market drop experienced in 2001.

FIXED INDEXED ANNUITIES – LIKE A CD WITH AN EARNINGS BOOST

Fixed Indexed Annuities are such a specialized type of annuity, they can be thought of as a CD with an earnings boost. They were once referred to as Equity Indexed Annuities, or EIAs, but have been reframed to be called FIAs. The key to how well these annuities perform has to do with a strategy known as indexing. The annuity is keyed to an equity index such as the S&P 500 so it can mirror the performance of that index, without participating directly in the equity investment. If the index does experiences a loss, your money is protected because the interest crediting rate is generally based on investments with known interest rates, such as bonds and certificates of deposit (CDs.) This growth limitation is balanced by the indexing factor, linking it to a certain degree of stock market growth. Your bottom line: growth with protection of principal, guaranteed. Like a CD with an earnings boost.

THE BENEFITS OF FIAS

Annuities can offer the income dependability of a pension controlled and administered by you. This gives you greater flexibility: you choose the amount of money you put in, when to turn on the income stream, and for how long. Additionally, you may be able to reduce the amount of fees and charges inside your current accounts by transferring your retirement savings from a company-sponsored plan to an individual annuity of your choosing. If creating a stable income is one of your retirement goals, consider the following benefits offered by the Fixed Indexed Annuity solution.

- **Guarantee of Principal:** not only is the amount you contribute to your annuity guaranteed, so is any interest credited on that principal. That means you can't lose money when the market drops. The worse thing that can happen during a stock market downturn is your account balance stays the same.

- **Minimum Guaranteed Cash Value:** Also known as a MGCV, means that you are assured of getting at least your entire contributed premiums back plus interest.

- **No Fees:** Indexed annuities rarely deduct fees from your account value. It's important to distinguish the difference between indexed annuities and variable annuities that typically *do* charge fees – even if the value of your account goes down. For example, the basic expense risk charges and administrative fees associated with a variable annuity average around 1.4 percent. Underlying subaccounts also carry their own fees, which average another 1 percent, and if you add that to an income rider or death benefit, the fees on a variable annuity can exceed 4 percent per year.

The fees on most FIAs are zero, unless select riders are added to the account.

- **Access to Your Money:** Many people think that you can't get to your principal with an annuity, but FIAs do offer some liquidity. Most of the FIA annuities allow you to withdraw up to 10 percent of the base amount after the first year without any penalty or surrender charges. That means if you have a $100,000 annuity, and after the first year you realize your house needs some significant repairs, you can take out $10,000 from that annuity without being penalized.

- **Additional Interest Credits:** Many FIA issuers offer additional interest credits based on a percent of your contribution. This additional interest credit or free money is credited to your account and added directly to your principal. The amount of the credit could be anywhere from 2 to 10 percent and varies from company to company, but it can be a nice way to recapture some of your stock market loss. For example, the maximum additional credit amount on a $500,000 principal deposit would be $50,000, for a total deposit of $550,000, which would begin earning interest and significantly increase the value of your FIA.

- **Tax Deferral:** All annuities grow their cash value on a tax-deferred basis. This means you can earn interest on that money without having it count against you as "earned interest" on your annual tax return. This allows your money to grow faster because no current taxes will be due until you begin taking payments (called "annuitizing"). Once the annuity is annuitized, a portion of each payment you receive will be tax free if the money you put into the contract came from income that was already taxed. When you receive payments, you will pay taxes on any pre-tax money you contributed and any interest earned in the annuity that is distributed to you.

- **Guaranteed Lifetime Income:** This is what FIAs do best – they give you a regular paycheck once you have stopped working. Lifetime income options vary depending on the FIA product and insurer, which is why it's important to discuss your options with a financial professional. FIAs offer several payout terms for a guaranteed number of years. For example, the annuity can be structured to provide income for the remainder of your lifetime, or for a certain number of years, or for the lifetime of two people.

WHY HAVEN'T I HEARD ABOUT THIS?

Some fixed indexed annuity products used to be a closed investments open only to millionaires. One such type of annuity, known as the Total Value Blended Index (TVBI) annuity, has only become opened to the average investor in recent years. Once known as "the billionaire's club," this brand of annuity is underwritten by the 120-year old company Guggenheim Securities, and Gradient is one of only four distributors in the U.S.

The TVBI is different from other indexed annuities in its blending of indexes. The TVBI is keyed to the top 100 stocks from the Dow and the S&P 500, as well as linked to treasury futures, global currencies and physical commodities such as energy, grains, industrial metals, livestock and natural gas. Because these are commodities that people around the world must consume, this stabilizes and balances the volatility. Typically what happens is that when the stock market goes down, commodities go up by about 20 percent. In this way, the TVBI annuity is able to offer an impressive growth rate that keeps up with inflation, while guaranteeing 100 percent of your principal. Remember, however, that these types of annuities are not appropriate for all investors.

HOW ANNUITIES WORK

So far, these new indexed annuities might sound a bit too good to be true. However, there is a method and a reason why these products work as well as they do. Remember, they were designed specifically to address the problem of lifetime income, during an era when fewer and fewer employers are offering pensions. When you place your lump sum into an annuity with an income rider, the plan is custom designed to address your ongoing income needs. The way that an annuity provides this income is due to the inner-working of the annuity, which can be explained by the following terms:

- **Annuity Roll Up:** This feature on an annuity works very much like the "roll up" on your Social security benefit. You put aside a sum of money today to be drawn upon for income tomorrow. The longer you wait to start taking the income, the greater that income will be. However, with an annuity, you have more control over the income amount. A "roll up" type of income annuity increases the amount of available income by a set percentage every year. This increase continues to grow – much like a rolling snowball that gathers snow – until you decide to take that income. The "roll up" happens regardless of market performance, meaning you get the peace of mind knowing you can structure an income that exactly meets your future needs.

- **Indexing:** As discussed earlier, this term refers to the link an annuity has to a market index, such as the S&P 500. If the linked index experiences a gain, you are entitled to a share of that gain as dictated by the terms of your annuity contract. If the index experiences a loss, your account is protected against that loss. Indexed annuities are fixed annuities that give you the opportunity to earn more money than other safe, Protected Money options. You can think of them as a CD with an earnings boost.

- **Annual Reset:** This is the method most fixed-indexed annuities rely on to preserve the amount of earned interest. Each year on the anniversary of the annuity – meaning the actual day the annuity was purchased – any interest credited to your account is locked in. Once that interest amount is locked in, it cannot be lost, regardless of what the stock market does the next day. Annual reset can potentially reward you with higher credited interest than other methods used to calculate interest, especially if the market fluctuates. Another thing to keep in mind is that if the annuity never loses money, it doesn't have to make up for previous losses in order to earn additional interest. Every anniversary, the index's ending value becomes the next year's starting value.
- **Income Riders:** When you purchase an indexed annuity, you will have the option of adding what is known as an income rider to the policy. Income riders pay you a guaranteed set income amount for the period of time designated by you. Most riders increase the growth rate of your gains by a set percentage each year for the life of the contract. This is what's known as a "stacking roll up" because additional interest is earned, or stacked up, on top of the base product interest rate. The fee for this rider varies by product, but is usually about one percent of the annuity value. The percentage of growth and the guaranteed income percentage are based on your age at the time you elect to receive the income payments. Safety and guarantees are based on the claims paying ability of the company and terms of the contract being honored. Surrender charges or a penalty for early withdrawal may apply.
- **Linked Benefits and LTC Riders:** Just like an income rider, a long term care rider can be added to your annuity

at the time of its purchase. Adding a long term care rider to your annuity can provide you or your spouse with an income doubler should one of you need to fund the cost of long term care during your lifetime. A linked benefit is another word for a long term care benefit, also known as Living Benefits. Living Benefits provide you with money *while you are still alive* to cover the expense of home health care and long term care. Many newer hybrid policies are being offered on traditional life insurance products as well, offering long term care benefits that can double the income of the policy holder to cover the cost of health care. Living Benefits on a life insurance policy may be harder to qualify for and dependent on your health history.

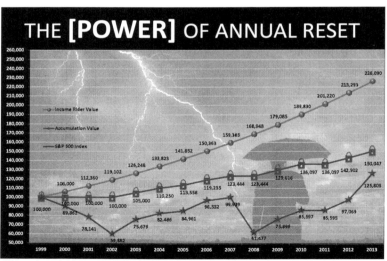

WHAT DOES AN ANNUITY INCOME LOOK LIKE?

Donna is 60 years old and is wondering how she can use her assets to provide her with a retirement income. She has a $5,000 per month income need. If she starts withdrawing her Social Security benefit in six years at age 66, it will provide her with $2,200 per month. She also has a pension that kicks in at age 70 that will give her another $1,320 per month.

That leaves an income gap of $2,800 from ages 66 to 69, and then an income gap of $1,480 at age 70 and beyond. If Donna uses only safe Know So Money vehicles to solve her income need, she will need to deposit $918,360 at 2 percent interest to meet her monthly goal for her lifetime. If she opts to use Hope So Money in risk vehicles and withdraws the amount she needs each month from the market, let's say the S & P 500, she will run out of cash in 10 years (if, for example, she had invested between the years of 2000 and 2012). Suffering a market downturn like that during the period for which she is relying on it for retirement income will change her life, and not for the better.

Working with a financial professional to find a better way, Donna found that she could take a hybrid approach to fill her income gap. Her professional recommended two different income vehicles: one that allowed her to deposit just $190,161 with a 2 percent return, and one that was a $146,000 income annuity. These tools filled her income gap with $336,161, requiring her to spend $582,000 less money to accomplish her goal! Working with a professional to find the right tools for her retirement needs saved Donna over half a million dollars.

Creating an income plan before you retire allows you to satisfy your need for lifetime income and ensures that your lifestyle can last as long as you do. You also want to create a plan that operates in the most efficient way possible. Doing so will give more security to your Leave On Money and will potentially allow you to build your legacy down the road.

The purpose of the money you've worked so hard to build up and grow is to provide you with a regular income. Leaving that large sum in growth vehicles means you will still be charged fees, and still lose money when interest rates drop, without the benefit of additional deposits and thirty or so more years of growth. Creating a regular income stream from a lump sum of money connected to the stock market is not only risky, but complicated. Leaving your money at risk means your income is at risk. How great or how bad the market is performing means nothing to you when you are trying to pay your bills and buy your groceries. Like Joe and Victoria at the beginning of the chapter, you need a reliable amount of income regardless of what the stock market is doing. You need an investment tool that is *just right*. The Fixed Indexed Annuity is such a financial tool. It offers growth, flexibility, and protection, and is designed to provide you with a steady income – for life.

CHAPTER 6 RECAP //

- Many retirees struggle to find an investment tool that is "just right" during their retirement years. Typical interest rates on safe, Protected Money don't earn enough to keep pace with inflation and taxes, while money left in the market can potentially devastate your retirement income.

- Today's new annuities are designed to protect your retirement savings in any market. They offer flexibility, protection, and a guaranteed income.

- An FIA is a Fixed Indexed Annuity, previously known as an EIA or Equity Indexed Annuity, is a special type of annuity that is keyed to the performance of the stock market. It offers growth with a guarantee safety of your principal, making it behave like a CD with an earnings boost.

- The benefits of an FIA include: guarantee of principal, a minimum guaranteed cash value, no fees, access to your money, bonus money, tax deferral, and a guaranteed lifetime income.

- Certain brands and types of indexed annuities, such as the Total Value Blended Index Annuity, have been previously unavailable to the average investor. The TVBI annuity is keyed to market commodities such as livestock and minerals, making these products more stable and able to earn stronger returns. Remember, these annuities may not be appropriate for everyone.

- The inner workings of annuities include "roll ups," indexing, annual reset, income riders (which act like a "stacking roll up") and linked benefits which can provide Living Benefits such as funding for long term care.

- Be sure you understand the features, benefits, costs and fees associated with any annuity product before you invest.

7

Liquidity and Your Three Buckets

"What if I need my money?"

Hank is a corn and soybean farmer with 1,200 acres of land. He routinely retains somewhere between $40,000 and $80,000 in his checking and savings accounts. If a major piece of equipment fails and needs repair or replacement, Hank will need the money available to pay for the equipment and carry on with farming. If the price of feed for his cattle goes up one year, he will need to compensate for the increased overhead to his farming operation. He isn't a particularly wealthy farmer, but he has little choice but to keep a portion of money on hand in case something comes up and he must access it quickly. Most of his capital is held in livestock in the pasture or crops in the ground tied up for six to eight months of the year. When a major financial need arises, Hank can't just harvest 10 acres of soybeans and *use them for payment. He needs to depend heavily on Liquidity in order to be a successful farmer.*

Old habits die hard, however, and when Hank finally hangs up his overalls and quits farming, he keeps his bank accounts flush with cash, just like in the old days. After selling the farm and the equipment, Hank keeps a huge portion of the profits in Liquid investments because that's what he is familiar with. Unfortunately for Hank, with his pile of money sitting in his checking account, he isn't even keeping pace with inflation. After all his hard work as a farmer, his money is losing value every day because he didn't shift to a paradigm of leveraging his assets to generate income and accumulate value.

Almost anything would be a better option for Hank than clinging to Liquidity. He could have done something better to get either more return from his money or more safety, and at the very least would not have lost out to inflation.

Throughout the book, we have discussed how today, investment options require advice that is relevant to today. Traditional, outdated investment strategies are not only ineffective; they can be harmful to the average investor. One of the most traditional ways of thinking about investing is the risk versus reward trade-off. It goes something like this:

Investment options that are considered safer carry less risk, but also offer the potential for less return. Riskier investment options carry the burden of volatility and a greater potential for loss, but they also offer a greater potential for large rewards. Most professionals move their clients back and forth along this range, shifting between investments that are safer and investments that are structured for growth. Essentially, the old rules of investing dictate that you can either choose relative safety *or* return, but you can't have both.

Updated investment strategies work with the flexibility of liquidity to remake the rules. Here is how:

There are three dimensions that are inherent in any investment: *Liquidity, Safety,* and *Return.* You can maximize any two of these dimensions at the expense of the third. If you choose Safety and Liquidity, this is like keeping your assets in a checking account or savings account. This option delivers a lot of Safety and Liquidity, but at the expense of any Return. On the other hand, if you choose Liquidity and Return, meaning you have the potential for great return and can still reclaim your money whenever you choose, you will likely be exposed to a very high level of risk.

Understanding Liquidity can help you break the old Risk versus Safety trade-off. By identifying assets from which you don't require Liquidity, you can place yourself in a position to potentially profit from relatively safe investments that provide a higher than average rate of return.

Choosing Safety and Return over Liquidity can have significant impacts on the accumulation of your assets. In the example story of Hank and his liquid investment portfolio, the paradigm shift from earning and saving to leveraging assets was a costly one.

YOUR THREE BUCKETS

This solution to the liquidity/safety/return dilemma is an important part of income planning because people are living longer now than they used to. The importance of income planning is more important now than ever before, because those Leave On dollars have to stretch further into the future. One solution to this dilemma is the structuring of three separate accounts, organized with your short and long term objectives in mind.

As yourself, how much Liquidity do you *really* need?

If you haven't sat down and created an income plan for your retirement, your perceived need for Liquidity is a guess. You don't know how much cash you'll need to fill the income gap if you don't know the amount of your Social Security benefit or the total of your other income options. If you *have* determined your income needs and have made a plan for filling your income gap, you can partition your assets based on when you will need them.

Bucket #1 Liquidity account for short-term needs: The money is placed in a checking account, savings, or money market account. If the brakes go out on your car, you will have the peace of mind in knowing that the $600 for repairs is there. Meeting regularly with your financial professional will ensure that the account is replenished as needed.

Bucket #2 Intermediate account for 5 to 7 year needs: Depending on your age, this money could be invested in CDs at the bank, a life insurance policy where you can take the money out tax free, or an indexed annuity. Ideally, you want to "set it and forget it" when it comes to your Leave On money.

Bucket #3 Long Term Buckets: This is money designed for income needs 10 plus years out. It could be your IRA money rolled over into a mix of index annuities for the long term. With IRA accounts, you don't want to have to take the money out until age 70.5 years of age because the withdrawal will trigger taxation on the amount you withdraw. These are the accounts we rebalance to provide safety, security, growth and guarantees. Again the thinking here for your long term, Leave On Money is: "Bull or Bear, you don't care."

Taking control of your assets and protecting your nest egg is where the muscle of your plan really goes to work for you. As you set your plan into motion, it's important to revisit the plan at least annually. Your financial professional should stay in touch with you to make adjustments, re-strategize, and fine-tune your plan as life events such as weddings, births, divorce, and new cars come into play. When these life-events crop up, it's important to pull the needed funds from the right bucket in order to avoid costly mistakes to your retirement assets.

CHAPTER 7 RECAP //

- A three-bucket approach to your money can provide liquidity when you need it, and growth for long term income. This will help ensure that your money lasts as long as you do.

8

Reducing Taxes During Retirement

"Will I be taxed on my Social Security income?"

Taxes play a starring role in the theater of retirement planning. Everyone is familiar with taxes (you've been paying them your entire working life), but not everyone is familiar with how to make tax planning a part of their retirement strategy, and specifically that Social Security is subject to income taxes.

Taxes are taxes, right? You'll pay them before retirement and you'll pay them during retirement. What's the difference? The truth is that a planful approach to taxes can help you save money, protect your assets and ensure that your legacy remains intact.

How can a tax form do all that? The answer lies in planning. **Tax planning** and **tax reporting** are two very different things. Most people only *report* their taxes. March rolls around, people pull out their 1040s or use TurboTax to enter their income and taxable assets, and ship it off to Uncle Sam at the IRS. If you use a CPA to report your taxes, you are essentially paying them to record history. You have the option of being proactive with your taxes and to plan for your future by making smart, informed decisions about how taxes affect your overall financial plan. Working with a financial professional who, along with a CPA, makes recommendations about your finances to you, will keep you looking forward instead of in the rearview mirror as you enter retirement.

TAXES AND RETIREMENT

When you retire, you move from the earning and accumulation phase of your life into the asset distribution phase of your life. For most people, that means relying on Social Security, a 401(k), an IRA, or a pension. Wherever you have put your Know So Money for retirement, you are going to start relying on it to provide you with the income that once came as a paycheck. Most of these distributions will be considered income by the IRS and will be taxed as such. There are exceptions to that (not all of your Social Security income is taxed, and income from Roth IRAs is not taxed), but for the most part, your distributions will be subject to income taxes.

Regarding assets that you have in an IRA or a 401(k) plan that uses an IRA, when you reach 70 ½ years of age, you will be required to draw a certain amount of money from your IRA as income each year. That amount depends on your age and the balance in your IRA. The amount that you are required to withdraw as income is called a Required Minimum Distribution (RMD). Why are you required to withdraw money from your own account? Chances are the money in that account has grown over time, and the government wants to collect taxes on that growth. If you have a large balance in an IRA, there's a chance your RMD could increase your income significantly enough to put you into a higher tax bracket, subjecting you to a higher tax rate.

Here's where tax planning can really begin to work strongly in your favor. In the distribution phase of your life, you have a predictable income based on your RMDs, your Social Security benefit and any other income-generating assets you may have. What really impacts you at this stage is how much of that money you keep in your pocket after taxes. Essentially, *you will make more money saving on taxes than you will by making more money.* If you can reduce your tax burden by 30, 20 or even 10 percent, you earn yourself that much more money by not paying it in taxes.

How do you save money on taxes? By having a plan. In this instance, a financial professional can work with the CPAs at their firm to create a distribution plan that minimizes your taxes and maximizes your annual net income.

BUILDING A TAX DIVERSIFIED PORTFOLIO

So far so good: avoid taxes, maximize your net annual income and have a plan for doing it. When people decide to leverage the experience and resources of a financial professional, they may not be thinking of how distribution planning and tax planning will benefit their portfolios. Often more exciting prospects like planning income annuities, investing in the market and structuring investments for growth rule the day. Taxes, however, play a crucial role in retirement planning. Achieving those tax goals requires knowledge of options, foresight and professional guidance.

Finding the path to a good tax plan isn't always a simple task. Every tax return you file is different from the one before it because things constantly change. Your expenses change. Planned or unplanned purchases occur. Health care costs, medical bills, an inheritance, property purchases, reaching an age where your RMD kicks in or travel, any number of things can affect how much income you report and how many deductions you take each year.

Preparing for the ever-changing landscape of your financial life requires a tax-diversified portfolio that can be leveraged to balance the incomes, expenditures and deductions that affect you each year. A financial professional will work with you to answer questions like these:

- What does your tax landscape look like?
- Do you have a tax-diversified portfolio robust enough to adapt to your needs?
- Do you have a diversity of taxable and non-taxable income planned for your retirement?
- Will you be able to maximize your distributions to take advantage of your deductions when you retire?
- Is your portfolio strong enough and tax-diversified enough to adapt to an ever-changing (and usually increasing) tax code?

» When Darlene returned home after a week in the hospital recovering from a knee replacement, the 77-year-old called her daughter, sister and brother to let them know she was home and feeling well. She also should have called her CPA. Darlene's medical expenses for the procedure, her hospital stay, her medications and the ongoing physical therapy she attended amounted to more than $50,000.

*Currently, Americans can deduct medical expenses that are more than 7.5 percent of their Adjusted Gross Income (AGI). Darlene's AGI was $60,000 the year of her knee replacement, meaning she would be able to deduct $44,000 of her medical bills from her taxes that year. Her AGI dictated that she could deduct more than 80 percent of her medical expenses that year. **Darlene didn't know this**.*

Had she been working with a financial professional who regularly asked her about any changes in her life, her spending, or her expenses (expected or unexpected), Darlene could have saved thousands of dollars. Darlene can also file an amendment to her tax return to recoup the overpayment.

This relatively simple example of how tax planning can save you money is just the tip of the iceberg. No one can be expected to know the entire U.S. tax code. But a professional who is working with a team of CPAs and financial professionals have an advantage over the average taxpayer who must start from square one on their own every year. Have you been taking advantage of all the deductions that are available to you?

PROACTIVE TAX PLANNING

The implications of proactive tax planning are far reaching, and are larger than many people realize. Remember, doing your taxes in January, February, March or April means you are writing a history book. Planning your taxes in October, November or December means that you are writing the story as it happens. You can look at all the factors that are at play and make decisions that will impact your tax return before you file it.

Realizing that tax planning is an aspect of financial planning is an important leap to make. When you incorporate tax planning into your financial planning strategy, it becomes part of the way you maximize your financial potential. Paying less in taxes means you keep more of your money. Simply put, the more money you keep, the more of it you can leverage as an asset. This kind of planning can affect you at any stage of your life. If you are 40 years old, are you contributing the maximum amount to your 401(k) plan? Are you contributing to a Roth IRA? Are you finding ways to structure the savings you are dedicating to your children's education? Do you have life insurance? Taxes and tax planning affects all of these investment tools. Having a relationship with a professional who works with a CPA can help you build a truly comprehensive financial plan that not only works with your investments, but also shapes your assets to find the most efficient ways to prepare for tax time. There may be years that you could benefit from higher distributions because of the tax bracket that you are in, or there could be years you would benefit from taking less. There may be years when you have a lot of deductions and years you have relatively few. Adapting your distributions to work in concert with your available deductions is at the heart of smart tax planning. Professional guidance can bring you to the next level of income distribution, allowing you to remain flexible enough to maximize your tax efficiency. And remember, saving money on taxes makes you more money than making money does.

What you have on paper is important: your assets, savings, investments, which are financial expression of your work and time. It's just as important to know how to get it off the paper in a way that keeps most of it in your pocket. Almost anything that involves financial planning also involves taxes. Annuities, investments, IRAs, 401(k)s, 403(b), and many other investment options will have tax implications. Life also has a way of throwing curveballs. Illness, expensive car repair or replacement, or ***any event that has a financial impact on your life will likely have a corresponding tax implication*** around which you should adapt your financial plan. Tax planning does just that.

One dollar can end up being less than 25 cents to your heirs.

> » *When Peter's father passed away, he discovered that he was the beneficiary of his father's $500,000 IRA. Peter has a wife and a family of four children, and he knew that his father had intended for a large portion of the IRA to go toward funding their college educations.*
>
> *After Peter's father's estate is distributed, Peter, who is*

50 years old and whose two oldest sons are entering college, liquidates the IRA. By doing so, his taxable income for that year puts him in a 39.6 percent tax bracket, immediately reducing the value of the asset to $302,000. An additional

3.8 percent surtax on net investment income further diminishes the funds to $283,000. Liquidating the IRA in effect subjects much of Peter's regular income to the surtax, as well. At this point, Peter will be taxed at 43.4 percent.

Peter's state taxes are an additional 9 percent. Moreover, estate taxes on Peter's father's assets will claim another 22 percent. By the time the IRS is through, Peter's income from the IRA will be taxed at 75 percent, leaving him with $125,000 of the original $500,000. While it would help contribute to the education of his children, it wouldn't come anywhere near completely paying for it, something the $500,000 could have easily done.

As the above example makes clear, leaving an asset to your beneficiaries can be more complicated than it may seem. In the case of a traditional IRA, after federal, estate and state taxes, the asset could literally diminish to as little as 25 percent of its value.

How does working with a professional help you make smarter tax decisions with your own finances? Any financial professional worth their salt will be working with a firm that has a team of trained tax professionals, including CPAs, who have an intimate knowledge of the tax code and how to adapt a financial plan to it.

Here's another example of how taxes have major implications on asset management:

» *Greg and Rhonda, a 62-year-old couple, begin working with a financial professional in October. After structuring their assets to reflect their risk tolerance and creating assets that would provide them Know So Money income during retirement, they feel good about their situation. They make decisions that allow them to maximize their Social Security benefits, they have plenty of options for filling their income gap, and have begun a safe yet ambitious Leave On Money strategy with their professional. When their professional asks them about their tax plan, they tell him their CPA handled their taxes every year, and did a great job. Their professional says, "I don't mean who does your taxes, I mean, who does your tax planning?" Greg and Rhonda aren't sure how to respond.*

Their professional brings Greg and Rhonda's financial plan to the firm's CPA and has her run a tax projection for them. A week later their professional calls them with a tax plan for the year that will save them more than $3,000 on their tax return. The couple is shocked. A simple piece of advice from the CPA based on the numbers revealed that if they paid their estimated taxes before the end of the year, they would be able to itemize it as a deduction, allowing them to save thousands of dollars.

This solution won't work for everyone, and it may not work for Greg and Rhonda every year. That's not the point. By being proactive with their approach to taxes and using the resources made available by their financial professional, they were able to create a tax plan that saved them money.

ESTATE TAXES

The government doesn't just tax your income from investments while you're alive. They will also dip into your legacy.

While estate taxes aren't as hot of a topic as they were a few years ago, they are still an issue of concern for many people with assets. While taxes may not apply on estates that are less than $5 million, certain states have estate taxes with much lower exclusion ratios. Some are as low as $600,000. Many people may have to pay a state estate tax. One strategy for avoiding those types of taxes is to move assets outside of your estate. That can include gifting them to family or friends, or putting them into an irrevocable trust. Life insurance is another option for protecting your legacy.

THE BENEFITS OF DIVERSIFICATION

Heading into retirement, we should be situated with a diversified tax landscape. The point to spending our whole lives accumulating wealth is not to see the size of the number on paper, but rather to be an exercise in how much we put in our pocket after removing it from the paper. To truly understand tax diversification, we must understand what types of money exist and how each of these will be treated during accumulation and, most importantly, during distribution. The following is a brief summary:

1. Free money
2. Tax-advantaged money
3. Tax-deferred money
4. Taxable money
   a. Ordinary income
   b. Capital gains and qualified dividends

FREE MONEY

Free money is the best kind of money regardless of tax treatment because, in the end, you have more money than you would have otherwise. Many employers will provide contributions toward employee retirement accounts to offer additional employment benefits and encourage employees to save for their own retirement. With this, employers often will offer a matching contribution in which they contribute up to a certain percentage of an employee's salary (generally three to five percent) toward that employee's retirement account when the employee contributes to their retirement account as well. For example, if an employee earns $50,000 annually and contributes three percent ($1,500) to their retirement account annually, the employer will also contribute three percent ($1,500) to the employee's account. That is $1,500 in free money. Take all you can get! Bear in mind that any employer contribution to a 401(k) will still be subject to taxation when withdrawn.

TAX-ADVANTAGED MONEY

Tax-advantaged money is the next best thing to free money. Although you have to earn tax-advantaged money, you do not have to give part of it away to Uncle Sam. Tax-advantaged money comes in three basic forms that you can utilize during your lifetime; four if prison inspires your future, but we are not going to discuss that option.

One of the most commonly known forms of tax-advantaged money is municipal bonds, which earn and pay interest that could be tax-advantaged on the federal level, or state level, or both. There are several caveats that should be discussed with regard to the notion of tax-advantaged income from municipal bonds. First, you will notice that tax-advantaged has several flavors from the state and federal perspective. This is because states will generally tax the interest earned on a municipal bond unless the bond is offered from an entity located within that state. This severely limits the availability of completely tax-advantaged municipal bonds and constrains underlying risk and liquidity factors. Second, municipal bond interest is added back into the equation for determining your modified adjusted gross income (MAGI) for Social Security. This could push your income above a threshold and subject a portion of your Social Security income to taxation.

In effect, if this interest subjects some other income to taxation then this interest is truly being taxed.

Last, municipal bond interest may be excluded from the regular federal tax system, but it is included for determining tax under the alternative minimum tax (AMT) system. In its basic form, the AMT system is a separate tax system that applies if the tax computed under AMT exceeds the tax computed under the regular tax system. The difference between these two computations is the alternative minimum tax.

TAX-ADVANTAGED MONEY: ROTH IRA

Roth accounts are probably the single greatest tax asset that has come from Congress outside of life insurance. They are well known but rarely used. Roth IRAs were first established by the Taxpayer Relief Act of 1997 and named after Senator William Roth, the chief sponsor of the legislation. Roth accounts are simply an account in the form of an individual retirement account or an employer sponsored retirement account that allows for tax-advantaged growth of earnings and, thus, tax-advantaged income.

The main difference between a Roth and a traditional IRA or employer-sponsored plan lies in the timing of the taxation. We are all very familiar with the typical scenario of putting money away for retirement through an employer plan, whereby they deduct money from our paychecks and put it directly into a retirement account. This money is taken out before taxes are calculated, meaning we do not pay tax on those earnings today. A Roth account, on the other hand, takes the money after the taxes have been removed and puts it into the retirement account, so we do pay tax on the money today. The other significant difference between these two is taxation during distribution in later years. Regarding our traditional retirement accounts, when we take the money out later it is added to our ordinary income and is taxed accordingly. Additionally, including this in our income subjects us to the consequences mentioned above for municipal bonds with Social Security taxation, AMT, as well as higher Medicare premiums. A Roth on the other hand is distributed tax-advantaged and does not contribute toward negative impact items such as

Social Security taxation, AMT, or Medicare premium increases. It essentially comes back to us without tax and other obligations.

The best way to view the difference between the two accounts is to look at the life of a farmer. A farmer will buy seed, plant it in the ground, grow the crops and harvest it later for sale. Typically, the farmer would only pay tax on the crops that have been harvested and sold. But if you were the farmer, would you rather pay tax on the $5,000 of seed that you plant today or the $50,000 of crops harvested later? The obvious answer is $5,000 of seed today. The truth to the matter is that you are a farmer, except you plant dollars into your retirement account instead of seeds into the earth.

So why doesn't everyone have a Roth retirement account if things are so simple? There are several reasons, but the single greatest reason has been the constraints on contributions. If you earned over certain thresholds (MAGI over $125,000 single and $183,000 joint for 2012), you were not eligible to make contributions, and until last year, if your modified adjusted gross income (MAGI) was over $100,000 (single or joint), you could not convert a traditional IRA to a Roth. Outside these contribution limits, most people save for retirement through their employers and most employers do not offer Roth options in their plans. The reason behind this is because Roth accounts are not that well understood and people have been educated to believe that saving on taxes today is the best possible course of action.

TAX-ADVANTAGED MONEY: LIFE INSURANCE

As previously mentioned, the single greatest tax asset that has come from Congress outside of life insurance is the Roth account. Life insurance is the little-known or little-discussed tax asset that holds some of the greatest value in your financial history both during life and upon death. It is by far the best tax-advantaged device available. We traditionally view life insurance as a way to protect our loved ones from financial ruin upon our demise and it should be noted that everyone who cares about someone should have life insurance. Purchasing a life insurance policy ensures that our loved ones will receive income from the life insurance company to help them pay our final expenses and carry on with their lives without us comfortably when we die. The best part of the life insurance windfall is the fact that nobody will have to pay tax on the money received. This is the single greatest tax-advantaged device available, but it has one downside, we do not get to use it. Only our heirs will.

The little-known and discussed part of life insurance is the cash value build-up within whole life and universal life (permanent) policies. Life insurance is not typically seen as an investment vehicle for building wealth and retirement planning, although we should discuss briefly why this thought process should be re-evaluated. Permanent life insurance is generally misconceived as something that is very expensive for a wealth accumulation vehicle because there are mortality charges (fees for the death benefit) that detract from the available returns. Furthermore, those returns do not yield as much as the stock market over the long run. This is why many times you will hear the phrase "buy term and invest the rest," where "term" refers to term insurance.

Let us take a second to review two terms just used in regard to life insurance: term and permanent. Term insurance is an idea with which most people are familiar. You purchase a certain death benefit that will go to your heirs upon death and this policy will be in effect for a certain number of years, typically 10 to 20 years. The 10 to 20 years is the term of the policy and once you have reached that end you no longer have insurance unless you purchase another policy.

Permanent insurance on the other hand has no term involved. It is permanent as long as the premiums continue to be paid. Permanent insurance generally initially has higher premiums than term insurance for the same amount of death benefit coverage and it is this difference that is referred to when people say "invest the rest."

Simply speaking there are significant differences between these two policies that are not often considered when providing a comparative analysis of the numbers. One item that gets lost in the fray when comparing term and permanent insurance is that term usually expires before death. In fact, insurance studies show less than one percent of all term policies pay out death benefit claims. The issue arises when the term expires and the desire to have more insurance is still present.

A term policy with the same benefit will be much more expensive than the original policy and, many times, life events occur, such as cancer or heart conditions, which makes it impossible to acquire another policy and leaves your loved ones unprotected and tax-advantaged legacy planning out of the equation.

Another aspect and probably the most important piece in consideration of the future of taxation is the fact that permanent insurance has a cash accumulation value. Two aspects stand out with the cash accumulation value. First, as the cash accumulation value increases the death benefit will also increase whereas term insurance remains level. Second, this cash accumulation offers value to you during your lifetime rather than to your heirs upon death. The cash accumulation value can be used for tax-advantaged income during your lifetime through policy loans. Most importantly, this tax-advantaged income is available during retirement for distribution planning, all while offering the same typical financial protection to your heirs.

TAX-DEFERRED MONEY

Tax-deferred money is the type of money with which most of people are familiar, but we also briefly reviewed the idea above. Tax-deferred money is typically our traditional IRA, employer sponsored retirement plan or a non-qualified annuity. Essentially, you put money into an investment vehicle that will accumulate in value over time and you do not pay taxes on the earnings that grow these accounts until you distribute them. Once the money is distributed, taxes must be paid. However, the same negative consequences exist with regard to additional taxation and expense in other areas as previously discussed. The cash accumulation value can be used for tax-advantaged income.

TAXABLE MONEY

Taxable money is everything else and is taxable today, later or whenever it is received. These four types of money come down to two distinct classifications: taxable and tax-free. The greatest difference when comparing taxable and tax-advantaged income is a function of how much money we keep after tax. For help in determining what the differences should be, excluding outside factors such as Social Security taxation and AMT, a tax equivalent yield should be used.

TAX-ADVANTAGED IN THE REAL WORLD

To put the tax equivalent yield into perspective, let us look at an example: Bob and Mary are currently retired, living on Social Security and interest from investments and falling within the 25 percent tax bracket. They have a substantial portion of their investments in municipal bonds yielding 6 percent, which is quite comforting in today's market. The tax equivalent yield they would need to earn from a taxable investment would be 8 percent, a 2 percent gap that seems almost impossible given current market volatility. However, something that has never been put into perspective is that the interest from their municipal bonds is subject to taxation on their Social Security benefits (at 21.25 percent). With this, the yield on their municipal bonds would be 4.725

percent, and the taxable equivalent yield falls to 6.3 percent, leaving a gap of only 1.575 percent.

In the end, most people spend their lives accumulating wealth through the best, if not the only vehicle they know, a tax-deferred account. This account is most likely a 401(k) or 403(b) plan offered through our employer and may be supplemented with an IRA that was established at one point or another. As the years go by, people blindly throw money into these accounts in an effort to save for a retirement that we someday hope to reach.

The truth is, most people have an age selected for when they would like to retire, but spend their lives wondering if they will ever be able to actually quit working. To answer this question, you must understand how much money you will have available to contribute toward your needs. ***In other words, you need to know what your after-tax income will be during this period.***

All else being equal, it would not matter if you put your money into a taxable, tax-deferred or tax-advantaged account as long as income tax rates never change and outside factors are never an event. The net amount you receive in the end will be the same.

Unfortunately, this will never be the case. We already know that taxes will increase in the future, meaning we will likely see higher taxes in retirement than during our peak earning years.

Regardless, saving for retirement in any form is a good thing as it appears from all practical perspectives that future government benefits will be cut and taxes will increase. You have the ability to plan today for efficient tax diversification and maximization of our after-tax dollars during your distribution years.

CHAPTER 8 RECAP //

- Taxes play an important role during your retirement. It's important that you understand your obligations, and the differences between tax-deferred and tax-advantaged advantaged accounts.

- When you report your taxes, you are paying to record history. When you *plan* your taxes with a financial professional, you are proactively finding the best options for your tax return.

- Beginning at the age of 70.5, the Federal Government requires all IRA participants to take their RMD, or Required Minimum Distribution each year. Failure to take your RMD can cost you thousands of dollars in taxes and penalty fees.

- You make more money by saving on taxes than you do by making more money. This simple concept becomes extremely valuable to people in retirement and those living on fixed incomes.

- Tax planning can directly affect your beneficiaries, costing them or saving them hundreds of thousands of dollars. Converting from a traditional to a Roth IRA is one way to help preserve and build your legacy.

9

Taxes: Now or Later?

"How can I protect my beneficiaries from paying too much in taxes?"

Louis Brandeis provides one of the best examples illustrating how tax planning works. Brandeis was Associate Justice on the Supreme Court of the United States from 1916 to 1939. Born in Louisville, Kentucky, Brandeis was an intelligent man with a touch of country charm. He described tax planning this way:

"I live in Alexandria, Virginia. Near the Court Chambers, there is a toll bridge across the Potomac. When in a rush, I pay the dollar toll and get home early. However, I usually drive outside the downtown section of the city and cross the Potomac on a free bridge.

The bridge was placed outside the downtown Washington, D.C. area to serve a useful social service – getting drivers to drive the extra mile and help alleviate congestion during the rush hour.

If I went over the toll bridge and through the barrier without paying a toll, I would be committing tax evasion.

If I drive the extra mile and drive outside the city of Washington to the free bridge, I am using a legitimate, logical and suitable method of tax avoidance, and I am performing a useful social service by doing so.

*The tragedy is that **few people know that the free bridge exists.** "*

Like Brandeis, most American taxpayers have options when it comes to "crossing the Potomac," so to speak. It's a financial planner's job to tell you what options are available. You can wait until March to file your taxes, at which time you might pay someone to report and pay the government a larger portion of your income. However, you could instead file before the end of the year, work with your financial professional and incorporate a tax plan as part of your overall financial planning strategy. Filing later is like crossing the toll bridge. Tax planning is like crossing the free bridge. Which would you rather do?

The answer to this question is easy. Most people want to save money and pay less in taxes. What makes this situation really difficult in real life, however, is that the signs along the side of the road that direct us to the free bridge are not that clear. To normal Americans, and to plenty of people who have studied it, the U.S. tax code is easy to get lost in. There are all kinds of rules, exceptions to rules, caveats and conditions that are difficult to understand, or even to know about. What you really need to know is your options and the bottom line impacts of those options.

ROTH IRA CONVERSIONS

The attractive qualities of Roth IRAs may have prompted you to explore the possibility of moving some of your assets into a Roth account. Another important difference between the accounts is how they treat Required Minimum Distributions (RMDs). When you turn 70 ½ years old, you are required to take a minimum amount of money each year out of a traditional IRA. This amount is your RMD. It is treated as taxable income. Roth IRAs, however, do not have RMDs, and their distributions are not taxable. Quite a deal, right?

While having a Roth IRA as part of your portfolio is a good idea, converting assets to a Roth IRA can pose some challenges, depending on what kinds of assets you want to transfer.

One common option is the conversion of a traditional IRA to a Roth IRA. You may have heard about converting your IRA to a Roth IRA, but you might not know the full net result on your income. The main difference between the two accounts is that the growth of investments within a traditional IRA is not taxed until income is withdrawn from the account, whereas taxes are charged on contribution amounts to a Roth IRA, not withdrawals. The problem, however, is that when assets are removed from a traditional IRA, even if the assets are being transferred to a Roth IRA account, taxes apply.

There are a lot of reasons to look at Roth conversions. People have a lot of money in IRAs, up to multiple millions of dollars. Even with $500,000, when they turn 70.5 years old, their RMD is going to be $40,00 or $50,000, and they have to take that out whether they want to or not. It's a tax issue. Essentially, if you will be subject to high RMDs, it could have impacts on how much of your Social Security is taxable, and on your tax bracket.

By paying taxes now instead of later on assets in a Roth IRA, you can realize tax-advantaged growth. You pay once and you're done paying. Your heirs are done paying. It's a powerful tool. Here's a simple example to show you how powerful it can be:

Imagine that you pay to convert a traditional IRA to a Roth. You have decided that you want to put the money in a vehicle that gives you a tax-advantaged income option down the road. If you pay a

25 percent tax on that conversion and the Roth IRA then doubles in value over the next 10 years, you could look at your situation as only having paid 12.5 percent tax.

The prospect of tax-advantaged income is a tempting one. While you have to pay a conversion tax to transfer your assets, you also have turned taxable income into tax free retirement money that you can let grow as long as you want without being required to withdraw it.

There are options, however, that address this problem. Much like the Brandeis story, there may be a "free bridge" option for many investors.

Your financial professional will likely tell you that it is not a matter of whether or not you should perform a Roth IRA conversion, it is a matter of how much you should convert and when.

Here are some of the things to consider before converting to a Roth IRA:

- If you make a conversion before you retire, you may end up paying higher taxes on the conversion because it is likely that you are in some of your highest earning years, placing you in the highest tax bracket of your life. It is possible that a better strategy would be to wait until after you retire, a time when you may have less taxable income, which would place you in a lower tax bracket.

- Many people opt to reduce their work hours from full-time to part-time in the years before they retire. If you have pursued this option, your income will likely be lower, in turn lowering your tax rate.

- The first years that you draw Social Security benefits can also be years of lower reported income, making it another good time frame in which to convert to a Roth IRA.

One key strategy to handling a Roth IRA conversion is to *always be able to pay the cost of the tax conversion with outside money*. Structuring your tax year to include something like a significant deduction can help you offset the conversion tax. This way you aren't forced to take the money you need for taxes from the value of the IRA. The reason taxes apply to this maneuver is because when you withdraw money from a traditional IRA, it is treated as taxable income by the IRS. Your financial professional, with the help of the CPAs at their firm, may be able to provide you with options like after-tax money, itemized deductions or other situations that can pose effective tax avoidance options.

Some examples of avoiding Roth IRA conversions taxes include:

- *Using medical expenses that are above 10 percent of your Adjusted Gross Income.* If you have health care costs that you can list as itemized deductions, you can convert an amount of income from a traditional IRA to a Roth IRA that is offset by the deductible amount. Essentially, deductible medical expenses negate the taxes resulting from recording the conversion.

- *Individuals, usually small business owners, who are dealing with a Net Operating Loss (NOL).* If you have NOLs, but aren't able to utilize all of them on your tax return. You can carry them forward to offset the taxable income from the taxes on income you convert to a Roth IRA.

- *Charitable giving.* If you are charitably inclined, you can use the amount of your donations to reduce the amount of taxable income you have during that year. By matching the amount you convert to a Roth IRA to the amount your taxable income was reduced by charitable giving, you can essentially avoid taxation on the conversion. You may decide to double your donations to a charity in one year, giving them two years' worth of donations in order to offset the Roth IRA conversion tax on this year's tax return.

- *Investments that are subject to depletion.* Certain investments can kick off depletion expenses. If you make an investment and are subject to depletion expenses, they can be deducted and used to offset a Roth IRA conversion tax.

Not all of the above scenarios work for everyone, and there are many other options for offsetting conversion taxes. The point is that you have options, and your financial professional and tax professional can help you understand those options.

If you have a traditional IRA, Roth conversions are something you should look at. As you approach retirement you should consider your options and make choices that keep more of your money in your pocket, not the government's.

ADDITIONAL TAX BENEFITS OF ROTH IRAS

Not only do Roth IRAs provide you with tax-advantaged growth, they also give you a tax diversified landscape that allows you to maximize your distributions. Chances are that no matter the circumstances, you will have taxed income and other assets subject to taxation. ***But if you have a Roth IRA, you have the unique ability to manage your Adjusted Gross Income (AGI), because you have a tax-advantaged income option!***

Converting to a Roth IRA can also help you preserve and build your legacy. Because Roth IRAs are exempt from RMDs, after you make a conversion from a traditional IRA, your Roth account can grow tax-advantaged for another 15, 20 or 25 years and it can be used as tax-advantaged income by your heirs. It is important to note, however, that non-spousal beneficiaries do have to take RMDs from a Roth IRA, or choose to stretch it and draw tax-advantaged income out of it over their lifetime.

TO CONVERT OR NOT TO CONVERT?

Conversions aren't only for retirees. You can convert at any time. Your choice should be based on your individual circumstances and tax situation. Sticking with a traditional IRA or converting to a Roth, again, depends on your individual circumstances, including your income, your tax bracket and the amount of deductions you have each year.

Is it better to have a Roth IRA or traditional IRA? It depends on your individual circumstance. Some people don't mind having taxable income from an IRA. Their income might not be very high and their RMD might not bump their tax bracket up, so it's not as big a deal. A similar situation might involve income from Social Security. Social Security benefits are taxed based on other income you are drawing. If you are in a position where none or very little of your Social Security benefit is subject to taxes, paying income tax on your RMD may be very easy.

> » *There are also situations where leveraging taxable income from a traditional IRA can work to your advantage come tax time. For example, Darrel and Linda dream of buying a boat when they retire. It is something they have looked forward to their entire marriage. In addition to the savings and investments that they created to supply them with income during retirement, which includes a traditional IRA, they have also saved money for the sole purpose of purchasing a boat once they stop working.*
>
> *When the time comes and they finally buy the boat of their dreams, they pay an additional $15,000 in sales taxes that year because of the large purchase. Because they are retired and earning less money, the deductions they used to be able to realize from their income taxes are no longer there. The high amount of sales taxes they paid on the boat puts them in a*

position where they could benefit from taking taxable income from a traditional IRA.

When Darrel and Linda's financial professional learns about their purchase, he immediately contacts a CPA at his firm to run the numbers. They determine that by taking a $15,000 distribution from their IRA, they could fulfill their income needs to offset the $15,000 sales tax deduction that they were claiming due to the purchase of their boat. In the end, they pay zero taxes on their income distribution from their IRA.

The moral of the story? **Having a tax diversified landscape gives you options**. Having capital assets that can be liquidated, tax-advantaged income options and sources that can create capital gains or capital losses will put you in a position to play your cards right no matter what you want to accomplish with your taxes. The ace up your sleeve is your financial professional and the CPAs they work with. Do yourself a favor and *plan* your taxes instead of *reporting* them!

ROTH ALTERNATIVE

There is a product on the market that behaves very much like a super-charged Roth IRA. It allows you to make contributions at today's tax rate so you can pull it out later without being taxed. This product is an Indexed Universal Life Product or an IUL. You can put money into an IUL in the same way as with a Roth IRA. The difference is there are no limits to the amount of dollars you can put into an IUL. There are limits on a Roth.

Just like with a Roth IRA, you can redirect some of the money you've been tucking away into your 401(k) and opt for an IUL instead. Why would you want to do this? For one thing, you would enjoy the benefit of a tax-free retirement. And second, if anything happened to you before you cashed in on your savings, the death benefit on your IUL would pay out to your beneficiaries.

The IUL is a little-known alternative investment that gives you a tax advantaged retirement in addition to a fully-funded death benefit so your spouse or loved ones can still enjoy that same tax-free retirement should you meet an early demise. This investment is often a good option for people who are over-funding their 401(k). For example, if you are making $100,000 a year, and your company is matching 5 percent, then you're getting a free $5,000 employer contribution annually. If you are contributing $10,000 to that 401(k), you are over-funding, because there is no more free money available to you. A better option may be to take that additional $5,000 and redirect it into an alternative investment vehicle so you don't have all your eggs in one basket. An IUL is a good one to consider. It functions like a Roth IRA, giving you a tax-advantaged retirement with the added bonus of a fully-funded death benefit. Bear in mind that IULs, like any investment, are not suitable for every investor.

CHAPTER 9 RECAP //

- The future of U.S. taxation is uncertain. You know what the tax rate and landscape is today, but you won't tomorrow. The only thing you can really count on is the trend of increasing taxation.
- Look for the "free bridge" option in your tax strategy.
- Converting from a traditional to a Roth IRA can provide you with tax-advantaged retirement income and help you preserve and build your legacy.
- Tax planning can directly affect your beneficiaries, costing them or saving them hundreds of thousands of dollars. Converting from a traditional to a Roth IRA is one way to help preserve and build your legacy.
- Work with a financial professional to discover ways to make converting to a Roth IRA do-able by using sources of outside money to fund the tax payment that comes as part of the conversion.
- Consider an IUL as part of a diversified investment portfolio. IUL's work like a super-charged Roth IRA, allowing you to grow an unlimited amount of money today for a tax-free retirement tomorrow.

10

Maximize Your Legacy

"How much money can I leave my grandchildren?"

Mr. Smith has a daughter, Amy, who is putting herself through college. When Mr. Smith meets his demise due to brain cancer, he leaves Amy his IRA valued at $125,000. Amy would really like to cash that in and buy a new car. Her uncle, however, knows that her father did not intend for a large portion of his daughter's IRA to go toward paying taxes. He has Amy sit down with his financial professional. After some counsel, Amy realizes that her uncle is right: if she cashes in the IRA now and takes it as a lump sum, a large percentage of the IRA would go toward taxes because the distribution would put Amy in a much higher tax bracket.

Instead, the financial professional put the $125,000 into a Total Value Annuity. In 10 years, when Amy is 35, that annuity will be worth $250,000. When she is 45, it will be worth $500,000. At the age of 55, Amy will be a millionaire without ever having to put in *one more dime into the TVA annuity. When she retires at the age of 65, Amy will have an annuity worth $2 million dollars.*

While it seems pretty incredible that a $125,000 IRA can turn someone like Amy into a millionaire by the time she retires, the power of compound interest can really go to work for you if you start saving when you are young. The key to investing isn't how much, but how long. Teaching your children and grandchildren the importance of *Paying Yourself First* is perhaps one of the biggest lessons that must be learned for the retirees of the future.

If you are in your 20s, 30s, or 40s and reading this book, pay special attention: it is imperative that you get into the habit of tucking a little something away every week. Your company 401(k) won't be enough, and Social Security may or may not be there for you. If you don't pay yourself first, then you're really going to be in a pickle. If you are lucky enough to have someone leave you an inheritance, consider the strategy employed by Amy in the story example above, and use wise judgment when planning for your tomorrow.

PLANNING YOUR LEGACY

While estate planning may not be on the top of your list of things to do, the fact of the matter is that if you don't plan your legacy, someone else will. That someone else is usually a combination of the IRS and other government entities: lawyers, executors, courts, and accountants. Who do you think has the best interests of your beneficiaries in mind?

Today, there is more consideration given to planning a legacy than just maximizing your estate. When most people think about an estate, it may seem like something only the very wealthy have: a stately manor or an enormous business. But a legacy is something else entirely. A legacy is more than the sum total of the financial assets you have accumulated. It is the lasting impression you make on those you leave behind. The dollar and cents are just a small part of a legacy.

A legacy encompasses the stories that others tell about you, shared experiences and values. An estate may pay for college tuition, but a legacy may inform your grandchildren about the importance of higher education and self-reliance.

A legacy may also contain family heirlooms or items of emotional significance. It may be a piece of art your great-grandmother painted, family photos, or a childhood keepsake.

When you go about planning your legacy, certainly explore strategies that can maximize the financial benefit to the ones you care about. But also take the time to ensure that you have organized the whole of your legacy, and let that be a part of the last gift you leave.

Many people avoid planning their legacy until they feel they must. Something may change in your life, like the birth of a grandchild, the diagnosis of a serious health problem, or the death of a close friend or loved one. Waiting for tragedy to strike in order to get your affairs in order is not the best course of action. The emotional stress of that kind of situation can make it hard to make patient, thoughtful decisions. Taking the time to create a premeditated and thoughtful legacy plan will assure that your assets will be transferred where and when you want them when the time comes.

THE BENEFITS OF PLANNING YOUR LEGACY

The distribution of your assets, whether in the form of property, stocks, Individual Retirement Accounts, 401(k)s or liquid assets, can be a complicated undertaking if you haven't left clear instructions about how you want them handled. Not having a plan will cost more money and take more time, leaving your loved ones to wait (sometimes for years) and receive less of your legacy than if you had a clear plan.

Planning your legacy will help your assets be transferred with little delay and little confusion. Instead of leaving decisions about how to distribute your estate to your family, attorneys or financial professionals, preserve your legacy and your wishes by drafting a clear plan at an early age.

And while you know all that, it can still be hard to sit down and do it. It reminds you that life is short, and the relatively complicated nature of sorting through your assets can feel like a daunting task. But one thing is for sure: ***it is impossible for your assets to be transferred or distributed the way you want at the end of your life if you don't have a plan.***

Ask yourself:

- Is my asset inventory up to date?
- Have my primary and contingent beneficiaries been clearly designated?
- Does my plan allow for restriction of a beneficiary?
- Does my legacy plan address minor children that I want to provide with income?
- Does my legacy plan allow for multi-generational payout?
- Answers to these questions are critical if you want the final say in how your assets are distributed. In order to achieve your legacy goals, you need a plan.

MAKING A PLAN

Eventually, when your income need is filled and you have sufficient standby money to meet your need for emergencies, travel or other extra expenses you are planning for, whatever isn't used during your lifetime becomes your financial legacy. The money that you do not use during your lifetime will either go to loved ones, unloved ones, charity, or the IRS. The question is, who would you rather disinherit?

By having a legacy plan that clearly outlines your assets, your beneficiaries and your distribution goals, you can make sure that

MAXIMIZE YOUR LEGACY

your money and property is ending up in the hands of the people you determine beforehand. Is it really that big of a deal? It absolutely is. Think about it. Without a clear plan, it is impossible for anyone to know if your beneficiary designations are current and reflect your wishes because you haven't clearly expressed who your beneficiaries are. You may have an idea of who you want your assets to go to, but without a plan, it is anyone's guess. It is also impossible to know if the titling of your assets is accurate unless you have gone through and determined whose name is on the titles. More importantly, *if you have not clearly and effectively communicated your desires regarding the planned distribution of your legacy, you and your family may end up losing a large part of it.*

As you can see, managing a legacy is more complicated than having an attorney read your will, divide your estate and write checks to your heirs. The additional issue of taxes, Family Maximum Benefit calculations and a host of other decisions rear their heads. Educating yourself about the best options for positioning your legacy assets is a challenging undertaking. Working with a financial professional who is versed in determining the most efficient and effective ways of preserving and distributing your legacy can save you time, money and strife.

So, how do you begin?

Making a Legacy Plan Starts with a Simple List. The first, and one of the largest, steps to setting up an estate plan with a financial professional that reflects your desires is creating a detailed inventory of your assets and debts (if you have any). You need to know what assets you have, who the beneficiaries are, how much they are worth and how they are titled. You can start by identifying and listing your assets. This is a good starting point for working with a financial professional who can then help you determine the

129

detailed information about your assets that will dictate how they are distributed upon your death.

If you are particularly concerned about leaving your kids and grandkids a lifetime of income with minimal taxes, you will want to discuss a Stretch IRA option with your financial professional.

MAXIMIZING YOUR IRA

In 1986, the U.S. Congress passed a law that allows for multi-generational distributions of IRA assets. This type of distribution is called a Stretch IRA because it stretches the distribution of the account out over a longer period of time to several beneficiaries. It also allows the account to continue accumulating value throughout your relatives' lifetimes. You can use a Stretch IRA as an income tool that distributes throughout your lifetime, your children's lifetimes and your grandchildren's lifetimes.

Stretch IRAs are an attractive option for those more concerned with creating income for their loved ones than leaving them with a lump sum that may be subject to a high tax rate. With traditional IRA distributions, non-spousal beneficiaries must generally take distributions from their inherited IRAs, whether transferred or not, within five years after the death of the IRA owner. An exception to this rule applies if the beneficiary elects to take distributions over his or her lifetime, which is referred to as stretching the IRA.

Unfortunately, many things play a role in failing to stretch IRA distributions. It can be tempting for a beneficiary to take a lump sum of money despite the tax consequences. Fortunately, if you want to solidify your plan for distribution, there are options that will allow you to open up an IRA and incorporate "spendthrift" clauses for your beneficiaries. This will ensure your legacy is stretched appropriately and to your specifications. Only certain insurance companies allow this option, and you will not find this benefit with any brokerage accounts. You need to work with a financial professional who has the appropriate relationship with an insurance company that provides this option.

Let's begin by looking at the potential of stretching an IRA throughout multiple generations.

> » *In this scenario, Mr. Cleaver has an IRA with a current balance of $350,000. If we assume a five percent annual rate of return, and a 28% tax rate, the Stretch IRA turned a $502,625 legacy into more than $1.5 million. Doubling the value of the IRA also provided Mr. Cleaver, his wife, two*

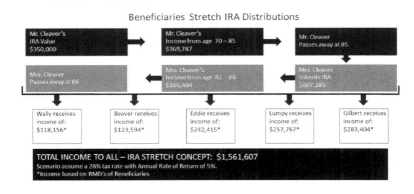

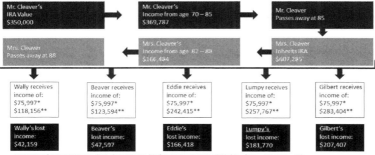

children and three grandchildren with income. Not choosing the stretch option would have cost nearly $800,000 and had impacts on six of Mr. Cleaver's loved ones.

Unfortunately, many things may also play a role in failing to stretch IRA distributions. It can be tempting for a beneficiary to take a lump sum of money despite the tax consequences. Fortunately, if you want to solidify your plan for distribution, there are options that will allow you to open up an IRA and incorporate "spendthrift" clauses for your beneficiaries. This will ensure your legacy is stretched appropriately and to your specifications. Only certain insurance companies allow this option, and you will not find this benefit with any brokerage accounts. You need to work with a financial professional who has the appropriate relationship with an insurance company that provides this option.

CHAPTER 10 RECAP //

- Tomorrow's retirees need to get into the habit of Paying Yourself First because Social Security and pensions may not be a reliable source of income. Maximizing an inheritance can be one way to fund your future retirement.

- Failing to maximize your retirement nest egg is a legacy planning mistake that can cost your beneficiaries thousands of dollars. With the counsel of a financial professional, it's possible to structure your assets in ways that maximize distributions to your beneficiaries, but for best results, the plan must be made before you pass away.

- It is your responsibility to designate your IRA as a Beneficiary IRA, also known as a "Stretch IRA." This designation, when done by you, ensures that income will be provided to you, your spouse, and your children and grandchildren. Stretch IRAs give beneficiaries the option of taking smaller distributions over the course of their lifetime, which allows them to take advantage of interest compounding over several years.

11

Your Living Trust: How to Avoid Probate, Save Taxes and More

David organized his assets long ago. He started planning his retirement early and made investment decisions that would meet his needs. With a combination of IRA to Roth IRA conversions, a series of income annuities and a well-planned money management strategy overseen by his financial professional, he easily filled his income gap and was able to focus on ways to accumulate his wealth throughout his retirement. He reorganized his Know So and Hope So Money as he got older. When David retired, he had an income plan created that allowed him to maximize his Social Security benefit. He even had enough to accumulate wealth during his retirement. At this point, David turned his attention to planning his legacy. He wanted to know how he could maximize the amount of his legacy he will pass on to his heirs.

David met with an attorney to draw up a will, but he quickly learned that while having a will was a good plan, it wasn't the most efficient way to distribute his legacy. In fact, relying solely on a will created several roadblocks.

The two main problems that arose for David were *Probate* and *Unintentional Disinheritance*:

Problem #1: Probate

Probate. Just speaking the word out loud can cause shivers to run down your spine. Probate's ugly reputation is well deserved. It can be a costly, time consuming process that diminishes your estate and can delay the distribution of your estate to your loved ones. Nasty stuff, by any measure. Unless you have made a clear legacy plan and discussed options for avoiding probate, it is highly likely that you have many assets that might pass through probate needlessly. ***If your will and beneficiary designations aren't correctly structured, some of these assets will go through the probate process, which can turn dollars into cents.***

If you have a will, probate is usually just a formality. There is little risk that your will won't be executed per your instructions. The problem arises when the costs and lengthy timeline that probate creates come into play. Probate proceedings are notoriously expensive, lengthy and ponderous. A typical probate process identifies all of your assets and debts, pays any taxes and fees that you owe (including estate tax), pays court fees, and distributes your property and assets to your inheritors. This process usually takes at least a year, and can take even longer before your inheritors actually receive anything that you have left for them. For this reason, and because of the sometimes exorbitant fees that may be charged by lawyers and accountants during the process, probate has earned a nasty reputation.

Probate can also be a painstakingly public process. Because the probate process happens in court, the assets you own that go through a probate procedure become part of the public record. While this may not seem like a big deal to some, other people don't want that kind of intimate information available to the public.

Additionally, if your estate is entirely distributed via your will, the money that your family may need to cover the costs of your medical bills, funeral expenses and estate taxes will be tied up in probate, which can last up to a year or more. While immediate family members may have the option of requesting immediate cash from your assets during probate to cover immediate health care expenses, taxes, and fees, that process comes with its own set of complications. Choosing alternative methods for distributing your legacy can make life easier for your loved ones and can help them claim more of your estate in a more timely fashion than traditional methods.

A simpler and less tedious approach is to avoid probate altogether by structuring your estate to be distributed outside of the probate process. Two common ways of doing this are by structuring your assets inside a life insurance plan, and by using individual retirement planning tools like IRAs that give you the option of designating a beneficiary upon your death.

Problem #2: Unintentionally Disinheriting Your Family

You would never want to unintentionally disinherit a loved one or loved ones because of confusion surrounding your legacy plan. Unfortunately, it happens. Why? This terrible situation is typically caused by a simple lack of understanding. In particular, mistakes regarding legacy distribution occur with regards to those whom people care for the most: their grandchildren.

One of the most important ways to plan for the inheritance of your grandchildren is by properly structuring the distribution of your legacy. Specifically, you need to know if your legacy is going to be distributed *per stirpes* or *per capita*.

Per Stirpes. *Per stirpes* is a legal term in Latin that means "by the branch." Your estate will be distributed *per stirpes* if you designate each branch of your family to receive an equal share of your estate. In the event that your children predecease you, their share will be distributed evenly between their children — your grandchildren.

Per Capita. *Per capita* distribution is different in that you may designate different amounts of your estate to be distributed to members of the same generation.

Per stirpes distribution of assets will follow the family tree down the line as the predecessor beneficiaries pass away. On the other hand, per capita distribution of assets ends on the branch of the family tree with the death of a designated beneficiary. For example, when your child passes away, in a per capita distribution, your grandchildren would not receive distributions from the assets that you designated to your child.

What the terms mean is not nearly as important as what they do, however. The reality is that improperly titled assets could accidentally leave your grandchildren disinherited upon the death of their parents. It's easy to check, and it's even easier to fix.

A simple way to remember the difference between the two types of distribution goes something like this: "***Stripes are forever and Capita is capped.***"

Another way to avoid complicated legacy distribution problems, and the probate process, is by leveraging a life insurance plan.

DIFFRENCE BETWEEN A WILL AND A LIVING TRUST

Unlike a will, which does not automatically avoid probate when you die, a Living Trust transfers assets from your name to the name of your trust. This is something that you can control while you are living, so that when you die, the courts cannot take control of your assets.

A will provides no protection to your assets until after you die, so if you become incapacitated or mentally unable to make decisions at the end of your life, your assets will be at risk. A Living Trust allows you to keep full control of your assets although legally, you no longer own those assets. Your assets belong to your trust. This simple concept is what keeps you and your family out of the courts. If you can no longer conduct business due to dementia, a stroke, or other ailment, a Living Trust is a legal document that contains your instructions.

Many types of trusts exists, and each with its own pros and cons. A financial advisor can help you determine which kind of trust offers the best terms for your situation.

LIFE INSURANCE: AN IMPORTANT LEGACY TOOL

One of the most powerful legacy tools you can leverage is a good life insurance policy. Life insurance is a highly efficient legacy tool because it creates money when it is needed or desired the most. Over the years, life insurance has become less expensive, while it offers more features, and it provides longer guarantees.

There are many unique benefits of life insurance that can help your beneficiaries get the most out of your legacy. Some of them include:

- Providing beneficiaries with a tax-free, liquid asset.
- Covering the costs associated with your death.
- Providing income for your dependents.
- Offering an investment opportunity for your beneficiaries.
- Covering expenses such as tuition or mortgage down payments for your children or grandchildren.

Very few people want life insurance, but nearly everyone wants what it does. Life insurance is specifically, and uniquely, capable of creating money when it is needed most. When a loved one passes, no amount of money can remove the pain of loss. And certainly, money doesn't solve the challenges that might arise with losing someone important.

It has been said that when you have money, you have options. When you don't have money, your options are severely limited. You might imagine a life insurance policy can give your family and loved ones options that would otherwise be impossible.

> » *Ben spent the last 20 years building a small business. In so many ways, it is a family business. Each of his three children, Maddie, Ruby and Edward, worked in the shop part-time during high school. But after all three attended college, only Maddie returned to join her father, and eventually will run the business full-time when Ben retires.*
>
> *Ben is able to retire comfortably on Social Security and on-going income from the shop, but the business is nearly his entire financial legacy. It is his wish that Maddie own the business outright, but he also wants to leave an equal legacy to each of his three children.*
>
> *There is no simple way to divide the business into thirds and still leave the business intact for Maddie.*
>
> *Ben ends up buying a life insurance policy to make up the difference. Ruby and Edward will receive their share of an inheritance in cash from the life insurance policy and Maddie will be able to inherit the business intact.*
>
> *Ben is able to accomplish his goals, treat all three children equitably and leave Maddie the business she helped to build.*

If you have a life insurance policy but you haven't looked at it in a while, you may not know how it operates, how much it is worth and how it will be distributed to your beneficiaries. You may also need to update your beneficiaries on your policy. In short, without a comprehensive review of your policy, you don't really know where the money will go or to whom it will go.

If you don't have a life insurance policy but are looking for options to maintain and grow your legacy, speaking with a professional can show you the benefits of life insurance. Many people don't consider buying a life insurance policy until some event in their life triggers it, like the loss of a loved one, an accident or a health condition.

BENEFITS OF LIFE INSURANCE

Life insurance is a useful and secure tool for contingency planning, ensuring that your dependents receive the assets that you want them to have, and for meeting the financial goals you have set for the future. While it bears the name "Life Insurance," it is, in reality, a diverse financial tool that can meet many needs. The main function of a life insurance policy is to provide financial assets for your survivors. Life insurance is particularly efficient at achieving this goal because it provides a tax-advantaged lump sum of money in the form of a death benefit to your beneficiary or beneficiaries. That financial asset can be used in a number of ways. It can be structured as an investment to provide income for your spouse or children, it can pay down debts, and it can be used to cover estate taxes and other costs associated with death.

Tax liabilities on the estate you leave behind are inevitable. Capital property, for instance, is taxed at its fair market value at the time of your death, unless that property is transferred to your spouse. If the property has appreciated during the time you owned it, taxation on capital gains will occur. Registered Retirement Savings Plans (RRSPs) and other similarly structured assets are also included as taxable income unless transferred to a beneficiary as well. Those are just a few examples of how an estate can become subject to a heavy tax burden. The unique benefits of a life insurance policy provide ways to handle this tax burden, solving any liquidity problems that may arise if your family members want to hold onto an illiquid asset, such as a piece of property or an investment. Life insurance can provide a significant amount of money to a family member or other beneficiary, and that money is likely to remain exempt from taxation or seizure.

One of life insurance's most important benefits is that it is not considered part of the estate of the policy holder. The death benefit that is paid by the insurance company goes exclusively to the beneficiaries listed on the policy. This shields the proceeds of the policy from fees and costs that can reduce an estate, including probate proceedings, attorneys' fees and claims made by creditors. The distribution of your life insurance policy is also unaffected by delays of the estate's distribution, like probate. Your beneficiaries will get the proceeds of the policy in a timely fashion, regardless of how long it takes for the rest of your estate to be settled.

Investing a portion of your assets in a life insurance policy can also protect that portion of your estate from creditors. If you owe money to someone or some entity at the time of your death, a creditor is not able to claim any money from a life insurance policy or an annuity, for that matter. An exception to this rule is if you had already used the life insurance policy as collateral against a loan. If a large portion of the money you want to dedicate to your legacy is sitting in a savings account, investment or other liquid form, creditors may be able to receive their claim on it before your beneficiaries get anything, that is if there's anything left. A life insurance policy protects your assets from creditors and ensures that your beneficiaries get the money that you intend them to have.

HOW MUCH LIFE INSURANCE DO YOU NEED?

Determining the type of policy and the amount right for you depends on an analysis of your needs. A financial professional can help you complete a needs analysis that will highlight the amount of insurance that you require to meet your goals. This type of personalized review will allow you to determine ways to continue providing income for your spouse or any dependents you may have. A financial professional can also help you calculate the amount of income that your policy should replace to meet the needs of your beneficiaries and the duration of the distribution of that income.

You may also want to use your life insurance policy to meet any expenses associated with your death. These can include funeral costs, fees from probate and legal proceedings, and taxes. You may also want to dedicate a portion of your policy proceeds to help fund tuition or other expenses for your children or grandchildren. You can buy a policy and hope it covers all of those costs, or you can work with a professional who can calculate exactly how much insurance you need and how to structure it to meet your goals. Which would you rather do?

AVOIDING POTENTIAL SNAGS
There are benefits to having life insurance supersede the direction given in a will or other estate plan, but there are also some potential snags that you should address to meet your wishes. For example, if your will instructs that your assets be divided equally between your two children but your life insurance beneficiary is listed as just one of the children, the assets in the life insurance policy will only be distributed to the child listed as the beneficiary. The beneficiary designation of your life insurance supersedes your will's instruction. This is important to understand when designating beneficiaries on a policy you purchase. Work with a professional to make sure that your beneficiaries are accurately listed on your assets, especially your life insurance policies.

USING LIFE INSURANCE TO BUILD YOUR LEGACY

Depending on your goals, there are strategies you can use that could multiply how much you leave behind. Life insurance is one of the most surefire and efficient investment tools for building a substantial legacy that will meet your financial goals.

Here is a brief overview of how life insurance can boost your legacy:

- Life insurance provides an immediate increase in your legacy.
- It provides an income tax-advantaged death benefit for your beneficiaries.
- A good life insurance policy has the opportunity to accumulate value over time.
- It may have an option to include long-term care (LTC) or chronic illness benefits should you require them.

If your Live On Money income needs for retirement are met and you have Leave On assets that will provide for your future expenses, you may have extra assets that you want to earmark as legacy funds. By electing to invest those assets into a life insurance policy, you can immediately increase the amount of your legacy. Remember, life insurance allows you to transfer a tax-advantaged lump sum of money to your beneficiaries. It remains in your control during your lifetime, can provide for your long-term care needs and bypasses probate costs. And make no mistake, taxes can have a huge impact on your legacy. Not only that, income and assets from your legacy can have tax implications for your beneficiaries, as well.

Here's a brief overview of how taxes could affect your legacy and your beneficiaries:

- The higher your income, the higher the rate at which it is taxed.
- Withdrawals from qualified plans are taxed as income.

- What's more, when you leave a large qualified plan, it ends up being taxed at a high rate.
- If you left a $500,000 IRA to your child, they could end up owing as much as $140,000 in income taxes.
- However, if you could just withdraw $50,000 a year, the tax bill might only be $10,000 per year.

How could you use that annual amount to leave a larger legacy? Luckily, you can leverage a life insurance policy to avoid those tax penalties, preserving a larger amount of your legacy and freeing your beneficiaries from an added tax burden.

» *When Brenda turned 70 years old, she decided it was time to look into life insurance policy options. She still feels young, but she remembers that her mother died in early 70s, and she wants to plan ahead so she can pass on some of her legacy to her grandchildren just like her grandmother did for her.*

Brenda doesn't really want to think about life insurance, but she does want the security, reliability and tax-advantaged distribution that it offers. She lives modestly, and her Social Security benefit meets most of her income needs. As the beneficiary of her late husband's Certificate of Deposit (CD), she has $100,000 in an account that she has never used and doesn't anticipate ever needing since her income needs were already met.

After looking at several different investment options with a professional, Brenda decides that a Single Premium life insurance policy fits her needs best. She can buy the policy with a $100,000 one-time payment and she is guaranteed that it would provide more than the value of the contract to her beneficiaries. If she left the money in the CD, it would be subject to taxes. But for every dollar that she puts into the *life insurance policy, her beneficiaries are guaranteed at least that dollar plus a death benefit, and all of it will be **tax-free!***

For $100,000, Brenda's particular policy offers a $170,000 death benefit distribution to her beneficiaries. By moving the $100,000 from a CD to a life insurance policy, Brenda increases her legacy by 70 percent. Not only that, she has also sheltered it from taxes, so her beneficiaries will be able to receive $1.70 for every $1.00 that she entered into the policy! While buying the policy doesn't allow her to use the money for herself, it does allow her family to benefit from her well-planned legacy.

MAKE YOUR WISHES KNOWN

Estate taxes used to be a much hotter topic in the mid-2000s when the estate tax limits and exclusions were much smaller and taxed at a higher rate than today. In 2008, estates valued at $2 million or more were taxed at 45 percent. Just two years later, the limit was raised to $5 million dollars taxed at 35 percent. The limit has continued to rise ever since. The limit applies to fewer people than before. Estate organization, however, is just as important as ever, and it affects everyone.

Ask yourself:

- Are your assets actually titled and held the way you think they are?
- Are your beneficiaries set up the way you think they should be?
- Have there been changes to your family or those you desire as beneficiaries?

There is more to your legacy beyond your property, money, investments and other assets that you leave to family members, loved ones and charities. Everyone has a legacy beyond money. You also leave behind personal items of importance, your values and beliefs, your personal and family history, and your wishes. Beyond a will and a plan for your assets, it is important that you make your wishes known to someone for the rest of your personal legacy. When it comes time for your family and loved ones to make decisions after you are gone, knowing your wishes can help them make decisions that honor you and your legacy, and give meaning to what you leave behind. Your professional can help you organize.

Think about your:

- Personal stories / recollections
- Values
- Personal items of emotional significance
- Financial assets
- Do you want to make a plan to pass these things on to your family?

WORKING WITH A PROFESSIONAL

Part of using life insurance to your greatest advantage is selecting the policy and provider that can best meet your goals. Venturing into the jungle of policies, brokers and salespeople can be over-whelming, and can leave you wondering if you've made the best decision. Working with a trusted financial professional can help you cut through the red tape, the "sales-speak" and confusion to find a policy that meets your goals and best serves your desires for your money. If you already have a policy, a financial profes-sional can help you review it and become familiar with the policy's premium, the guarantees the policy affords, its performance, and its features and benefits. A financial professional can also help you make any necessary changes to the policy.

> » *When Cheryl turned 88, her daughter finally convinced her to meet with a financial professional to help her organize her assets and get her legacy in order. Although Cheryl is reluctant*

to let a stranger in on her personal finances, she ends up very glad that she did.

In the process of listing Cheryl's assets and her beneficiaries, her professional finds a man's name listed as the beneficiary of an old life insurance annuity that she owns. It turns out, the man is Cheryl's ex-husband who is still alive. Had Cheryl passed away before her ex-husband, the annuities and any death benefits that came with them, would have been passed on to her ex-husband. This does not reflect her latest wishes.

Things change, relationships evolve and the way you would like your legacy organized needs to adapt to the changes that happen throughout your life. There may be a new child or grandchild in your family, or you may have been divorced or remarried. A professional will regularly review your legacy assets and ask you questions to make sure that everything is up to date and that the current organization reflects your current wishes.

CHAPTER 11 RECAP //

- Working with a financial professional can help ensure that many of your assets avoid the ponderous and expensive probate process. A Living Trust may be the right financial tool to make sure your wishes are carried out should you be unable to manage your assets while you are still living. A Living Trust also avoids the lengthy and costly process of probate.

- A financial professional can help review the details of the assets you have designated to be a part of your legacy and make sure that you aren't unintentionally disinheriting your heirs.

- Life insurance provides the distribution of tax-free, liquid assets to your beneficiaries.

- Investing in a life insurance policy can significantly build your legacy.

- Organizing your estate will allow you to make sure your wishes are properly carried through.

- Understand if your assets will be distributed *per stirpes* or *per capita.*

- Working with a financial professional can help you select the policy that best meets your needs, or can help you fine tune your existing policy to better reflect your desires and intentions.

12

Choosing A Financial Professional

"Who can I trust?"

At this point, it should come as no surprise that working with a financial professional is one of the best things you can do for yourself and for your future. Your professional will provide you with advice and manage the personal assets that will supply your retirement income and contribute to your legacy. However, it's not about working with any financial professional; it's about working with the financial professional who is right for you. Consequently, the process of choosing a professional is one of the most important financial decisions you will make in your life.

Remember Mark and Marie from the introduction? They were nearing retirement and looking forward to beginning the next phase of their life.

» Before they met with a financial professional, they had no idea what their retirement would look like. After they met with an agent, they knew exactly what types of assets they had, how much they were worth, how much risk they were exposed to, and how they were going to be distributed. They also created an income plan so that they could pay their bills every month the moment they retired, and they maximized their Social Security benefit by targeting the year and month they would get the most lifetime benefits. After their income needs were met, they were able to continue accumulating wealth by investing their extra assets to serve them in the future and contribute to their legacy. Their professional also helped them make decisions that impacted their taxes, protecting the value of their assets and allowing them to keep more of their money.

This isn't a fairy tale scenario. This is an example of how much you stand to gain by meeting with a financial professional who can help you create a purposeful approach that is uniquely suited to meeting your needs. From the moment you dip your toes into the retirement planning pool to the point you start swimming laps, your income needs met, your Live On and Leave On money balanced, and your health care and legacy plans in place, working with a professional that you trust can make all the difference in how well your retirement plan reflects your desires.

It is important to know what you are looking for before taking the plunge. Given all the financial components that your retirement plan will need to balance and address, it's easy to frame your plan solely through a financial perspective. However, it's crucial to remember that your retirement is ultimately determined by you: it doesn't matter how well your finances are structured if they don't support your future needs and goals. In other words, while there are many people that would love to work with your money and many of them are probably even qualified to do so, it's more important to find someone who you feel is qualified to work with *you*.

Finding the professional that's right for you is not a decision you can hand off to anyone else. The quality and security of your retirement depends on the investment strategies and asset structuring that you and your professional utilize. As a result, you need to bring your time and energy to the table when it comes to finding someone who will give you the personal attention and care required to help you overcome any obstacles you may face on your way to retirement.

HOW TO FIND A FINANCIAL PROFESSIONAL YOU CAN TRUST

You have probably realized that not all investment firms and financial professionals are created equal. There are a variety of different kinds of financial professionals, and you will need to decide which type is best suited to your particular situation. Some professionals specialize in particular areas of finance, while others might offer a more comprehensive outlook. There will probably be times when finding a good financial professional will feel like looking for a needle in a haystack. A good way to minimize this is by asking your friends, family, and colleagues for referrals.

You will want to pay particular attention to the recommendations that you get from others who are in your similar financial situation and who have similar lifestyle choices. The professional for the CEO of your company may have a different skill-set than the skill-set of the professional befitting your cousin who has three kids and a Subaru like you. Try to ask questions that will help you identify the overarching investment philosophies of the professional because this will tell you a lot about how they will handle your money.

However, asking for referrals can be a bit of a dangerous game because everyone has a recommendation about how you should manage your money and who should manage it for you. From hot stock tips to "the best money manager in the state," people love to share good information that makes them look like they are in-the-know. Nobody wants to talk about the bad stock purchases they made, the times they lost money, or the poor selections they made regarding financial professionals or stock brokers. If you decide to take a friend or family member's recommendation, make sure they have a substantial, long-term experience with the financial professional and that their glowing review isn't just based on a one-time "win."

One way to check the reliability of a referral is to call the professional directly and ask for references. Every professional should be able to provide you with at least two or three names. In fact, they will probably be eager to share them with you. Most professionals rely on references for validation of their success, quality of services, and likability. Asking questions will help give you a sense of how well the reference knows their professional and whether or not they are a quality reference.

You have seen that leveraging investments for income and accumulation in today's market requires new ideas, modern planning, and an individually customized approach. You need innovative ideas to come up with creative solutions that will provide you with the retirement that you want.

In other words, just like Mark and Mary, you need to retire *just right*.

Finding the financial professional who feels like they were created for you is a critical component of any retirement. This means asking enough questions to make sure the professional you choose is appropriately and uniquely suited to helping you achieve your retirement goals. As we've previously acknowledged, this is no easy task but it is an incredibly important and worthwhile one. Luckily, you've read this book, and you now have the information and tools you need to be able to ask the questions that truly matter.

Now, it's time to discover if the questions we've helped you learn how to ask can be met with the answers you need. At Retirement Strategies and Solutions, we are committed to providing our clients with retirement plans that are uniquely attuned to satisfy the requirements of their situation. Can we fit your plan just right? Let's find out!

THE TOP FIVE QUESTIONS TO ASK YOUR FINANCIAL PROFESSIONAL

1. What are the financial services that you and your firm provide?

We provide a variety of financial services and products to help you protect your assets and ensure they will last throughout the entirety of your retirement. Every successful retirement plan has a solid legal and financial pillar in each of the following four areas: estate planning, financial planning, taxes, and health care and legacy planning.

As you know, the primary goal of your retirement is to reliably and sustainably satisfy your income needs. I have been licensed to sell health insurance, life insurance, and annuities since 1985, and have found these financial products to be essential components of many successful retirement income plans. Additionally, these products can also begin to help build your legacy and fortify your estate plan.

I also run several different reports to help you understand your debt and current investment holdings so we will have a clear picture of your financial state and I use proprietary software that will help us discover the exact time for you to file for Social Security so you will be able to maximize your lifetime benefits.

Retirement Strategies and Solutions also has incredibly solid partnerships with Gradient Investments, LLC, Global Financial Private Capital, LLC, and Stovall and Associates, Ltd. By drawing on the strength of these alliances, I am able to create plans that include the strategies and services necessary to thoroughly address the remaining two retirement pillars: tax planning and financial planning.

Stovall and Associates, Ltd. craft customized tax plans that will help you avoid excessive taxation and maximize your wealth for generations to come. Likewise, working with Gradient Investments and Global Financial Private Capital ensures that any investment strategies we select for your retirement plan will be professionally and actively managed when necessary.

2. What kinds of clients do you work with the most?

I specialize in working with individuals who are nearing retirement or who have already retired. As a result, I am particularly well-versed in the difficulties associated with this unique time. Many of my clients are in the same financial boat as you and, thanks to the 30 years of professional experience I have been navigating them, I am very familiar with these waters! I have helped hundreds of people learn how to confidently captain their retirement futures.

3. How do you remain in contact with your clients?

During the preliminary planning stages of your retirement, I often meet with clients in person. Sometimes these meetings take place at my office or I make a "house call" and meet you at the location that's most convenient for you. Once we have a plan in place, I stay in contact through email and send out newsletters to keep you apprised of any important industry developments.

Mostly, however, I let you set the pace when it comes to maintaining contact. Trust and dependability are the cornerstones of my business, which means you can be guaranteed that I will personally return and respond to any message you leave for me. So long as there is a phone that works in the world, I will always promptly return my clients' phone calls!

4. Are you my main contact, or do you work with a team?

I will certainly be your main contact, but my partnerships with Stovall and Associates, Gradient Investments, and Global Financial Private Capital may mean some of your plan will include contact with my associates at these firms. My connections with these firms are invaluable resources because it allows your plan to be as diverse and comprehensive as necessary to best satisfy your needs.

Ultimately, not only is it unlikely that you'll find a financial professional who has all the solutions to your problems immediately at their fingertips but it's also unnecessary. It's more important to choose professionals, like myself and Nancy, who will truly listen to your questions and know how to direct you to the answer.

5. How do you provide a unique experience for your clients?

When you decide to work with Retirement Strategies and Solutions, you are getting two dedicated individuals for the price of one. As a husband and wife team, Nancy and I are committed to taking the time to get to know you so we can truly understand your financial goals, and help you find and plan the path you need to achieve them. We will listen to your goals and assess your risk tolerance so we can be sure that your needs are matched with the appropriate financial retirement strategies.

Our business sense is honed by our extensive experience, intellect, integrity, compassion, and patience. We are intently devoted to being the financial professionals you can trust. Not only do we have access to the financial strategies and tools you need, but we will take the time to truly get to know you. We believe that while your money may be the means of your retirement plan, your satisfaction and future is the ends. As a result, instead of providing you with a pre-fabricated plan, we will work with you to build a comprehensive and reliable retirement strategy that is capable of adapting to fluctuations both in the market and in your life. We will make sure that:

- Your assets are organized and structured to reflect your risk tolerance.
- Your assets will be available to you when you need them and in the way that you need them.
- You will have a lifetime income that will support your lifestyle through your retirement.
- You are handling your taxes as efficiently as possible.
- Your legacy is in order.
- You have both Live On and Leave On Money managed in your best interest.

THE JUST RIGHT PROFESSIONAL

Ultimately, you want to work with a financial professional who puts your interests first and actively wants to help you meet your goals and objectives. Oftentimes, the products someone sells you matter less than their dedication to making sure that you have a plan that meets your needs. Finding a professional who can do this is, in a nutshell, the difference between retiring and retiring the right way.

Most workers will eventually retire but, unfortunately, most of them won't retire the right way. Making sure you're included in the latter group means working with a financial professional who will help you create a plan that has been uniquely designed to fit your particular needs and goals. When it comes to retirement planning, what works for one person may not work for another. To put it more simply, there is no "one size fits all" strategy.

Just as Goldilocks wasn't satisfied until she tried the third bowl of porridge, perhaps you won't be satisfied with the first financial vehicle or strategy for retirement you encounter. In order to arrive at the retirement plan that is just right for you, you need a financial professional who understands your distinct situation and can provide you with a variety of potential solutions. Your professional should help you face the three bears of retirement and should never ask you to settle for a plan that doesn't fit you.

Moreover, you want a professional who takes your whole financial position into consideration and creates a plan that satisfies your income needs, mitigates your taxation, accounts for possible future healthcare costs, and begins building your legacy. For this plan to be successful, your professional needs to match your needs with the appropriate investment tools and financial products that may satisfy them. In other words, your retirement begins with you, which means your financial professional must begin with you, as well. Financial products and investment tools change, but the concepts that lie behind wise retirement planning are lasting. At Retirement Strategies and Solutions, you can rest assured we will be the financial professionals you want to help you satisfy your needs and achieve your goals.

When it comes down to it, planning your retirement can be a complicated process, but it doesn't have to be an overwhelming one. When you work with Nancy and me, you work with financial professionals you trust and you gain the peace of mind that comes with knowing you won't have to walk through the wilds of retirement alone. Today, you can make one of the best retirement decisions of your life by choosing to partner with us.

You are more than ready and capable to make this decision. Not only do you know how to look each of the three bears of retirement in the eye and address them head-on, but you've already confronted and defeated the biggest bear of them all: the procrastination bear. When you started this book, you were on the road to retiring. Now, however, you are on the road to retiring the right way. The difference is your future! Let us help take you the rest of the way home.

I always say, "Life is not a dress rehearsal: plan right and retire the right way."

CHAPTER 12 RECAP //

- A good financial professional puts your needs first. Your risk tolerance, goals, objectives, needs, wants, liquidity concerns, and timeline worries should be the focus of the meeting before they try to sell you any products. A plan is only good if it is a good fit for you and your family.

- Money isn't just about numbers, it's about the life events and people that come attached to those numbers. Consequently, it's imperative to find a financial professional you can trust.

- To find a professional you can trust, start by asking family and friends for referrals. Make sure to do your due diligence and check out the references of anyone who is recommended to you.

- When interviewing candidates, make sure you understand what services they offer and how they would fit into your financial plan for retirement. You want to ask enough questions so you can get a sense for who the professional is and how they conduct their business. Only then will you be able to know if they could be the financial professional who will help you create the retirement plan that is just right for you.

- The biggest mistake most people make when planning for retirement is not coming in soon enough to meet with a financial professional. Waiting until after you retire may mean that it will be too late to save lost money or correct irreversible money mistakes. Take a proactive approach and do the work now to find someone you can trust to secure the safety of your retirement nest egg BEFORE you retire. The peace of mind this will bring you just might be the most priceless asset of all.

- Jamie and Nancy Blumenthal boast over 30 years of professional experience in the financial industry helping retirees accomplish their retirement and estate planning goals. Their firm, Retirement Strategies and Solutions, is uniquely positioned to provide you with the tools and guidance you need to protect your assets, reliably satisfy your retirement income needs, and safeguard the tomorrow you deserve.

- Life is not a dress rehearsal: plan right and retire the right way!

GLOSSARY

ANNUAL RESET *(ANNUAL RATCHET, CLIQUET)* – Crediting methods measuring index movement over a one year period. Positive interest is calculated and credited at the end of each contract year and cannot be lost if the index subsequently declines. Say that the index increased from 100 to 110 in one year and the indexed annuity had an 80 percent participation rate. The insurance company would take the 10 percent gross index gain for the year (110-100/100), apply the participation rate (10 percent index gain x 80 percent rate) and credit 8 percent interest to the annuity. But, what if in the following year the index declined back to 100? The individual would keep the 8 percent interest earned and simply receive zero interest for the down year. An annual reset structure preserves credited gains and treats negative index periods as years with zero growth.

ANNUITANT – The person, usually the annuity owner, whose life expectancy is used to calculate the income payment amount on the annuity.

ANNUITY – An annuity is a contract issued by an insurance company that often serves as a type of savings plan used by individuals looking for long term growth and protection of assets that will likely be needed within retirement.

AVERAGING – Index values may either be measured from a start point to an end point (point-to-point) or values between the start point and end point may be averaged to determine an ending value. Index values may be averaged over the days, weeks, months or quarters of the period.

BENEFICIARY – A beneficiary is the person designated to receive payments due upon the death of the annuity owner or the annuitant themselves.

BONUS RATE – A bonus rate is the "extra" or "additional" interest paid during the first year (the initial guarantee period), typically used as an added incentive to get consumers to select their annuity policy over another.

CALL OPTION *(ALSO SEE PUT OPTION)* – Gives the holder the right to buy an underlying security or index at a specified price on or before a given date.

CAP – The maximum interest rate that will be credited to the annuity for the year or period. The cap usually refers to the maximum interest credited after applying the participation rate or yield spread. If the index methodology showed a 20 percent increase, the participation rate was 60 percent and the maximum interest cap was 10 percent, the contract would credit 10 percent interest. A few annuities use a maximum gain cap instead of a maximum interest cap with the participation rate or yield spread applied to the lesser of the gain or the cap. If the index methodology showed a 20 percent increase, the participation rate was 60 percent and the maximum gain cap was 10 percent, the contract would credit 6 percent interest.

COMPOUND INTEREST – Interest is earned on both the original principal and on previously earned interest. It is more favorable than simple interest. Suppose that your original principal was $1 and your interest rate was 10 percent for five years. With simple interest, your value is ($1 + $0.10 interest each year) = $1.50. With compound interest, your value is ($1 x 1.10 x 1.10 x 1.10

x 1.10 x 1.10) = \$1.61. The advantage of compound interest over simple interest becomes greater as each subsequent period passes.

CREDITING METHOD *(ALSO SEE METHODOLOGY)* – The formula(s) used to determine the excess interest that is credited above the minimum interest guarantee.

DEATH BENEFITS – The payment the annuity owner's estate or beneficiaries will receive if he or she dies before the annuity matures. On most annuities, this is equal to the current account value. Some annuities offer an enhanced value at death via an optional rider that has a monthly or annual fee associated with it.

EXCESS INTEREST – Interest credited to the annuity contract above the minimum guaranteed interest rate. In an indexed annuity the excess interest is determined by applying a stated crediting method to a specific index or indices.

FIXED ANNUITY – A contract issued by an insurance company guaranteeing a minimum interest rate with the crediting of excess interest determined by the performance of the insurer's general account. Index annuities are fixed annuities.

FIXED DEFERRED ANNUITY – With fixed annuities, an insurance company offers a guaranteed interest rate plus safety of your principal and earnings ((subject to the claims-paying ability of the insurance company). Your interest rate will be reset periodically, based on economic and other factors, but is guaranteed to never fall below a certain rate.

FREE WITHDRAWALS – Withdrawals that are free of surrender charges.

INDEX – The underlying external benchmark upon which the crediting of excess interest is based, also a measure of the prices of a group of securities.

IRA *(INDIVIDUAL RETIREMENT ACCOUNT)* – An IRA is a tax-advantaged personal savings plan that lets an individual set aside money for retirement. All or part of the participant's contributions may be tax deductible, depending on the type of IRA chosen and the participant's personal financial circumstances. Distributions from many employer-sponsored retirement plans may be eligible to be rolled into an IRA to continue tax-deferred growth until the funds are needed. An annuity can be used as an IRA; that is, IRA funds can be used to purchase an annuity.

IRA ROLLOVER – IRA rollover is the phrase used when an individual who has a balance in an employer-sponsored retirement plan transfers that balance into an IRA. Such an exchange, when properly handled, is a tax-advantaged transaction.

LIQUIDITY – The ease with which an asset is convertible to cash. An asset with high liquidity provides flexibility, in that the owner can easily convert it to cash at any time, but it also tends to decrease profitability.

MARKET RISK – The risk of the market value of an asset fluctuating up or down over time. In a fixed or fixed indexed annuity, the original principal and credited interest are not subject to market risk. Even if the index declines, the annuity owner would receive no less than their original principal back if they decided to cash in the policy at the end of the surrender period. Unlike a security, indexed annuities guarantee the original premium and the premium is backed by, and is as safe as, the insurance company that issued it (subject to the claims-paying ability of the insurance company).

METHODOLOGY *(ALSO SEE CREDITING METHOD)* – The way that interest crediting is calculated. On fixed indexed annuities, there are a variety of different methods used to determine how index movement becomes interest credited.

MINIMUM GUARANTEED RETURN *(MINIMUM INTEREST RATE)* – Fixed indexed annuities typically provide a minimum guaranteed return over the life of the contract. At the time that the owner chooses to terminate the contract, the cash surrender value is compared to a second value calculated using the minimum guaranteed return and the higher of the two values is paid to the annuity owner.

OPTION – A contract which conveys to its holder the right, but not the obligation, to buy or sell something at a specified price on or before a given date. After this given date the option ceases to exist. Insurers typically buy options to provide for the excess interest potential. Options may be American style whereby they may be exercised at any time prior to the given date, or they may have to be exercised only during a specified window. Options that may only be exercised during a specified period are European-style options.

OPTION RISK – Most insurers create the potential for excess interest in an indexed annuity by buying options. Say that you could buy a share of stock for $50. If you bought the stock and it rose to $60 you could sell it and net a $10 profit. But, if the stock price fell to $40 you'd have a $10 loss. Instead of buying the actual stock, we could buy an option that gave us the right to buy the stock for $50 at any time over the next year. The cost of the option is $2. If the stock price rose to $60 we would exercise our option, buy the stock at $50 and make $10 (less the $2 cost of the option). If the price of the stock fell to $40, $30 or $10, we wouldn't use the option and it would expire. The loss is limited to $2 – the cost of the option.

PARTICIPATION RATE – The percentage of positive index movement credited to the annuity. If the index methodology determined that the index increased 10 percent and the indexed annuity participated in 60 percent of the increase, it would be said that the contract has a 60 percent participation rate. Participation rates may also be expressed as asset fees or yield spreads.

POINT-TO-POINT – A crediting method measuring index movement from an absolute initial point to the absolute end point for a period. An index had a period starting value of 100 and a period ending value of 120. A point-to-point method would record a positive index movement of 20 [120-100] or a 20 percent positive movement [(120-100)/100]. Point-to-point usually refers to annual periods; however the phrase is also used instead of term end point to refer to multiple year periods.

PREMIUM BONUS – A premium bonus is additional money that is credited to the accumulation account of an annuity policy under certain conditions.

PUT OPTION *(ALSO SEE CALL OPTION)* – Gives the holder the right to sell an underlying security or index at a specified price on or before a given date.

QUALIFIED ANNUITIES *(QUALIFIED MONEY)* – Qualified annuities are annuities purchased for funding an IRA, 403(b) tax-deferred annuity or other type of retirement arrangements. An IRA or qualified retirement plan provides the tax deferral. An annuity contract should be used to fund an IRA or qualified retirement plan to benefit from an annuity's features other than tax deferral, including the safety features, lifetime income payout option and death benefit protection.

REQUIRED MINIMUM DISTRIBUTION *(RMD)* – The amount of money that Traditional, SEP and SIMPLE IRA owners and qualified plan participants must begin distributing from their retirement accounts by April 1 following the year they reach age 70.5. RMD amounts must then be distributed each subsequent year.

RETURN FLOOR – Another way of saying minimum guaranteed return.

ROTH IRA – Like other IRA accounts, the Roth IRA is simply a holding account that manages your stocks, bonds, annuities, mutual funds and CD's. However, future withdrawals (including earnings and interest) are typically tax-advantaged once the account has been open for five years and the account holder is age 59.5.

RULE OF 72 – Tells you approximately how many years it takes a sum to double at a given rate. It's handy to be able to figure out, without using a calculator, that when you're earning a 6 percent return, for example, by dividing 6 percent into 72, you'll find that it takes 12 years for money to double. Conversely, if you know it took a sum twelve years to double you could divide 12 into 72 to determine the annual return (6 percent).

SIMPLE INTEREST *(ALSO SEE COMPOUND INTEREST)* – Interest is only earned on the principal balance.

SPLIT ANNUITY – A split annuity is the term given to an effective strategy that utilizes two or more different annuity products – one designed to generate monthly income and the other to restore the original starting principal over a set period of time.

STANDARD & POOR'S 500 *(S&P 500)* – The most widely used external index by fixed indexed annuities. Its objective is to be a benchmark to measure and report overall U.S. stock market performance. It includes a representative sample of 500 common stocks from companies trading on the New York Stock Exchange, American Stock Exchange, and NASDAQ National Market System. The index represents the price or market value of the underlying stocks and does not include the value of reinvested dividends of the underlying stocks.

STOCK MARKET INDEX – A report created from a type of statistical measurement that shows up or down changes in a specific financial market, usually expressed as points and as a percentage, in a number of related markets, or in an economy as a whole (i.e. S&P 500 or New York Stock Exchange).

SURRENDER CHARGE – A charge imposed for withdrawing funds or terminating an annuity contract prematurely. There is no industry standard for surrender charges, that is, each annuity product has its own unique surrender charge schedule. The charge is usually expressed as a percentage of the amount withdrawn prematurely from the contract. The percentage tends to decline over time, ultimately becoming zero.

TRADITIONAL IRA – See IRA (Individual Retirement Account)

TERM END POINT – Crediting methods measuring index movements over a greater timeframe than a year or two. The opposite of an annual reset method. Also referred to as a term point-to-point method. Say that the index value was at 100 on the first day of the period. If the calculated index value was at 150 at the end of the period the positive index movement would be 50 percent (150-100/100). The company would credit a percentage of this movement as excess interest. Index movement is calculated and interest credited at the end of the term and interim movements during the period are ignored.

TERM HIGH POINT *(HIGH WATER MARK)* – A type of term end point structure that uses the highest anniversary index level as the end point. Say that the index value was at 100 on the first day of the period, reached a value of 160 at the end of a contract year during the period, and ended the period at 150. A term high point method would use the 160 value – the highest contract anniversary point reached during the period, as the end point and the gross index gain would be 60 percent (160-100/100). The company would then apply a participation rate to the gain.

TERM YIELD SPREAD – A type of term end point structure which calculates the total index gain for a period, computes the annual compound rate of return deducts a yield spread from the annual rate of return and then recalculates the total index gain for the period based on the net annual rate. Say that an index increased from 100 to 200 by the end of a nine year period. This is the equivalent of an 8 percent compound annual interest rate. If the annuity had a 2 percent term yield spread this would be deducted from the annual interest rate (8 percent-2 percent) and the net rate would be credited to the contract (6 percent) for each of the nine years. Total index gain may also be computed by using the highest anniversary index level as the end point.

VARIABLE ANNUITY – A contract issued by an insurance company offering separate accounts invested in a wide variety of stocks and/or bonds. The investment risk is borne by the annuity owner. Variable annuities are considered securities and require appropriate securities registration.

1035 EXCHANGE – The 1035 exchange refers to the section of tax code that allows annuity owners the flexibility to exchange one annuity for another without incurring any immediate tax liabilities. This action is most often utilized when an annuity holder decides they want to upgrade an annuity to a more favorable one, but they do not want to activate unnecessary tax liabilities that would typically be encountered when surrendering an existing annuity contract.

401(K) ROLLOVER – See <u>IRA Rollover</u>

35781129R00100

Made in the USA
Charleston, SC
18 November 2014